**Studio Spear**
PO Box 51291
Jacksonville Beach, FL 32240
www.studiospear.com

Published 2020

Printed in the United States

Designed by Studio Spear

ISBN 13: 978-0-9889191-1-2

Enjoy the adventure!

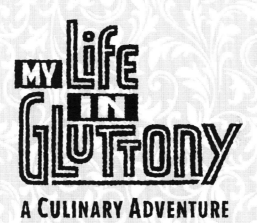

## A CULINARY ADVENTURE

WRITTEN & ILLUSTRATED BY
# JEFFREY SPEAR

---

**For Mom and Dad.
You made this book possible.**

---

# TABLE OF CONTENTS

**"Please sir, I want some more."**

*Oliver Twist*

 The notion of "living to eat" is no longer an admission of gluttony or a problem with self-control. It has, in fact, become a badge of honor.

There's no such thing as too much of a good thing. Whether we're talking about a big ol' pot of creamy mashed potatoes loaded with butter; a bubbling hot pan of crispy, brown-edged macaroni and cheese that's overflowing with extra sharp cheddar; an all-you-can-eat crab feast where the crabs are abundantly-spiced, heavy, and fat; a towering triple decker sandwich over-stuffed with corned beef, coleslaw, chopped liver, Swiss cheese, and Russian dressing; or an endless parade of Chinese ladies pushing dim sum carts filled with stacks and stacks of siu mai, har gow, wu gok, and char siu bao; all I can say is… bring it on!

I'm not exactly sure how this love affair with food got started but I have a pretty good idea. I blame it on my Mom.

Hortense Lee Spear, my mom, was a very good cook, especially when you consider that she, along with my Dad, raised my brother and me at a time when TV dinners and fast food were both coming into vogue. While she had no apprehensions about serving a Swanson's pot pie or heating up a can of Chef Boy-Ar-Dee ravioli (I used to love that stuff - ate it cold, right from the can for years), she made the majority of her dishes from scratch.

In particular, and to the family's delight, she loved to bake. On a regular basis, we were treated to cakes of all description as well as an impressive variety of fresh fruit pies (her pie crust is legendary). Needless to say, we ate well and enjoyed freshly prepared meals just about every day.

On weekends, and on those days when I was home from school, I was attracted to the curious noises and intoxicating aromas emanating from the kitchen. I was eager to see what Mom was up to and had to stick my nose and fingers into everything. Even when I wasn't in the kitchen, and usually around 4-o'clock in the afternoon while I was doing my homework, these gently seductive fragrances would sneak their way into my bedroom. Without fail, I'd call down to the kitchen "Hey Mom. Is dinner ready yet?"

While my parents were terrific, and there was never any doubt about their love or support for my brother or me, it must be said that I also found tremendous emotional satisfaction from a chunk of Hershey bar that I would steal from my Dad's stash in the pantry, or by secreting away any number of leftovers from the fridge.

With so much good food available at home, and little em-phasis placed on sports, outdoor adventure, or other such active pursuits, it's not surprising that I grew up as one of the fat kids in the neighborhood. I was teased, taunted, ignored, and overlooked. I was the kid that nobody wanted on their dodge-ball team, the outcast that was frequently exiled to the "geek" table during school lunches, and the oddball who earned hurtful nicknames including Tub o' Lard, Piggy, and Fatso. You get the idea.

Amidst all this taunting, one of the schoolyard bullies once asked, "Hey Spear, (feel free to replace Spear with any of the hurtful names previously mentioned), do you eat to live or live to eat?" While I did not fully understand the question (I was probably 12 years old at the time) and was not sure how to answer, I knew it was asked to make me feel badly about being overweight.

Lately, and having accumulated several decades of maturity under my belt, I can happily admit, without hesitation, that I live to eat.

There. I said it.

The good news is that I am not alone. Ever since the Food Network started entertaining us with exquisitely prepared meals, the ways in which people obtain, consume, and relate to food has changed. Culinary competitions have become regular fare for reality TV; celebrity chefs including Emeril (Bam!), Rachel (Yum-O!) and Bobby (Throwdown) dazzle us with their chops; and kitchen luminaries including Anthony Bourdain and Alton Brown have demonstrated a flair for writing that surpasses their skills in the kitchen. As a result, a significant percentage of Americans have declared their love for all things edible and become self-proclaimed foodies. Apparently, the notion of "living to eat" is no longer an admission of gluttony or a problem with self-control. It has, in fact, become a badge of honor.

Having a mother who was the best cook in the family, and the envy of many of her friends, meant I did not attempt to cook while still living under my parent's roof. In my early teens, however, and while I was in the Boy Scouts, I needed to demonstrate a basic facility with cooking in order to advance my First Class rank.

Out of all the recipes I found in the Scouting handbook, there were two that I felt I could manage. The first was Fruit Compote, which was basically dried fruit restored in boiling water with a little bit of added sugar for sweetness. The second was Tuna Noodle Casserole.

The compote was nothing to write home about. That being said, I fell in love with the casserole. It consisted of cooked wide noodles mixed with one can tuna (drained), one can cream of mushroom soup, and one can mixed vegetables (drained). All of this was placed in a pot, topped with some crumbled corn flakes for a crust, and heated over an open fire. It was delicious. In fact, when I returned home from the camp-out, I told my mom I wanted to have Tuna Noodle Casserole at home. She was appalled. Here she was, cooking from scratch and performing culinary magic for her family and her son wants Tuna Noodle Casserole! Sorry Mom.

From that day on, Tuna Noodle Casserole became a staple in my repertoire. And while I no longer recommend the original recipe, I have found several ways to make my favorite dish with a bit more sophistication.

It's clear that my Scouting adventure had a profound impact on my culinary preferences, especially my love for all things "noodle." That being said, I did not attempt to cook again until I left home for college.

In those days, being preoccupied with sex, drugs and rock and roll, my competency in the kitchen did not extend beyond scrambling eggs, making boxed macaroni and cheese, boiling water to cook noodles, and opening jars of spaghetti sauce. At the same time, however, I was taking note of the foods I encountered in restaurants, from street vendors, and at dinner parties in other people's homes. In short, I was slowly acquiring an informed and discriminating palate and learning quite a lot about ingredients, flavors, cooking styles, and methods of presentation.

Whether it was the pumpernickel bagel with lox and cream cheese I routinely purchased in New York's Penn Station during frequent visits to New York; the pecan pie that became a regular companion to my late night cups of coffee in various cafes and diners around Tucson; the nuances of the chili con carne that conspired with those wonderfully sloppy hamburgers, hot dogs and French fries I eagerly consumed in Los Angeles; or the dark, rich, and intensely flavorful flourless chocolate cakes I first encountered in Washington DC that made me wet my pants in public, I paid quite a lot of attention to food.

I moved to Los Angeles immediately after graduating from college and fell in with a crowd who enjoyed and pursued good food and stimulating culinary experiences. Together, we kept watch for the opening of all the new and groovy restaurants, were constantly eating out, would order way too much food, could not contain our animated outbursts when experiencing an edible masterwork, and were always on the lookout for the next great gastronomic encounter.

To my surprise, a few of my friends were very accomplished cooks. They were constantly reading and testing new recipes and throwing dinner parties. Recognizing that my culinary skills did not extend far beyond macaroni and cheese, and I could not yet contribute to the culinary discourse in any meaningful way, my invitations were limited.

There was an especially notable dinner party in San Francisco that stands out above the rest. It was obvious that, from the time we arrived until the time the desserts were served, the entire meal had been meticulously planned. The wines were expertly paired, timing was impeccable, and the overall impact was magnificent. When I mentioned how astonished I was with our host's culinary finesse, he revealed that all of the dishes, and many of the cooking tips he had come to trust, were obtained from the newly popular Silver Palate Cookbook.

Needless to say, and as soon as I returned home, I bought a copy and poured over its pages. This newfound treasure became my go-to resource for home cooked meals and became my sole reference when cooking for friends.

Having observed my mom in action, the kitchen was already a familiar place. I had a reasonable idea about the essential tools, the processes involved, and how to conduct myself without chopping off a finger or losing an eye. Now that I had discovered a reliable cookbook, the meals I prepared for myself became far better than anything I had made previously; and those I prepared for friends were met with rave reviews. Sadly, cooking was not yet something I found terribly enjoyable or wanted to do on a regular basis.

With the passing of time, nearly 35 years to be precise, my interest in food and patience in the kitchen has increased significantly, as have the number of cookbooks that line my kitchen shelves as reliable references and cooking companions.

More importantly, and while I continue to seek out great restaurants, enjoy having others cook for me, and still have a preference for macaroni and cheese (it remains one of my all-time favorite dishes - see Killer Macaroni & Cheese in the Jacksonville chapter), I have obtained a significant amount of culinary training and can work effortlessly in just about any kitchen. With a little bit of fooling around in commercial cooking environments, I have learned that I do not have the personality or spine to endure the rigors that the back-of-house demands. More importantly, I am confident that a career in foodservice would not end well.

My work as a food and beverage marketing consultant, however, is far more peaceful, can be performed while the sun shines, does not require cauldrons of sizzling hot oil, and has afforded me adventures in places I never knew existed.

Over the years, I've visited sunlight drenched and sweet smelling expanses of open farmland, orchards, and gardens as well as pulsating, cacophonous, and pungent, processing facilities where steel-toed shoes, lab coats and ear plugs are considered fashionable. Along the way, I've come to enjoy levels of hospitality and generosity of remarkable proportion, culinary experiences that have overwhelmed my senses, all of which has lifted my spirits in a manner that, for lack of better description, is comparable to falling in love.

Whenever others learn of my work, they ask about the places I've visited, the people I've met, and the foods I've encountered. When I reply, the undeniable truth becomes apparent - food has been an important facet of my life for many years and still is. In fact, most of my treasured memories include food in one form or another.

Since many of these experiences took place long before I had any interest in cooking, writing this book became an excuse to transfer memories to a more tangible format; to research the dishes I remember fondly, learn how to cook them, add some personal touches, and document them as properly formed recipes. Accordingly, a great deal of care was taken to ensure these formulas are flavorful, enjoyable, and bear a reasonable resemblance to some of the most enjoyable and remarkable meals I've ever had.

It is my hope that you will find this book entertaining and worthy of your time. Better still, I hope you'll find the recipes well written, easy to follow, and deliciously rewarding. If you enjoy entertaining as much as I do, it would be my recommendation to invite the people you love the most over to your place for tastings; making fond memories of your own along the way.

# SEAFOOD NOODLE CASSEROLE
Serves 4

---

*INGREDIENTS*
8 tablespoons butter, divided
1 cup onion, finely chopped
1 cup celery, finely chopped
1 red capsicum, finely chopped
1/4 cup flour
2 cups milk
1 teaspoon salt
1/2 teaspoon black pepper
1/2 lb. scallops
1/2 lb. shrimp (fully cleaned)
1/2 lb. cod fillets, cut into bite sized pieces
1 cup peas, fully cooked
1 lb. wide egg noodles
1/4 cup chopped parsley

DIRECTIONS
Melt 4 tablespoons of the butter in a Dutch oven over medium high heat. Stir in the onions, celery and capsicum and sauté for 5 minutes, then reduce the heat to low, cover and continue cooking for approximately 10 minutes longer, until the vegetables are fully cooked and soft.

Add the remaining 4 tablespoons of butter, then whisk in the flour, a little at a time to make a roux. When fully incorporated, slowly whisk in the milk, taking care to avoid lumps. Once a creamy sauce is achieved, add the salt and pepper.

Bring the sauce to a simmer, then gently add the scallops and shrimp and cook for 5 minutes. Add the fish and cook for another 10 minutes, stirring occasionally, taking care not to break up the seafood while stirring.

While the dish is cooking, bring a large pot of salted water to a boil. Cook the noodles until just tender, then drain.

To serve, distribute the noodles evenly in four bowls. Top with equal portions of the casserole and garnish with parsley.

---

*"I am not a glutton. I am an explorer of food."*
*Erma Bombeck*

---

 There must have been two hundred like-minded people cracking and hammering away at their crabs, all the while laughing, drinking, and spitting the night away.

**F**rom the time of my earliest memories, in spite of absolutely no interest in cooking, I loved being in the kitchen with my Mom. Don't ask me what she was doing or to accurately describe what she was making (I used to think that the egg whites she was beating into stiff peaks were whipped cream. I simply could not understand why she would always slap my hand away when I tried to sneak a taste). The bottom line is that I found tremendous pleasure and comfort being with her in the kitchen.

It's important to say that, while my Mom would serve us TV dinners, canned ravioli, and frequently relied on condensed soups for sauces, she made the majority of her meals from scratch and was considered the best cook in the family. Whether she was frying garlic and onions for chicken cacciatore, measuring flour, baking powder, and sugar for her sour cream based coffee cake, mixing up a batch of orgasmic marbled fudge bars, or rolling out dough for one of her sensational fruit pies, watching her chop, measure, sift, whip, fold, and assemble was always fascinating.

I especially loved watching her bake. While I was too young to have any idea what she was doing, I liked watching the electric mixer at work, the folding of ingredients, the changing colors and textures, and the aromatic magic that happened when the assembled product was subjected to heat in the oven. I also enjoyed (I'm sure most of you reading this book will understand) licking the remains that clung to the bowl, spatula, and beaters.

After all these years, little has changed. While my Mom is long-gone and I am the one making the cakes, muffins, cookies and pies, I still enjoy licking the bowl. If anyone is in the kitchen with me, it's even more fun to share.

While my culinary experiences at home were formative (and frequently quite delicious), there were many that took place away from home that remain some of the most eye opening, enjoyable, and cherished.

When you grow up in Maryland (I grew up on the edge of suburban Baltimore with a corn field in the back yard), you quickly learn that the state boasts a sizable agricultural community generating a delicious abundance of farm fresh products. You also find that, with the Chesapeake Bay as the most significant natural resource in the region, seafood influences what you have for dinner on a regular basis.

So, as the days got longer, the temperatures got warmer, and neighborhood kids on summer vacation started congregating at night to chase the lightning bugs, the harvests from local farms and the Bay became visibly apparent and quite abundant. Whether it was sweet white corn, luscious tomatoes, crisp green beans, juicy peaches, or ripe melons, roadside stands would overflow with just harvested fruits and vegetables that were second to none. When it came to seafood, along with oysters, clams, and a variety of fin fish, the seasonal indulgence was blue crab.

It's important to understand that Marylanders have a unique and passionate relationship with blue crab. To start, any crab that is not harvested from the Chesapeake or its tributaries is treated as second class. Then there's the method of preparation. From jumbo lump crab cakes and soft shelled crab sandwiches to steamed crabs and crab Imperial, there are as many variations as there are stars in the sky. The only ones that count, however, are the ones that adhere to certain unwritten, yet generally understood, Maryland standards.

To complicate matters, there are seafood restaurants and crab houses on just about every corner. Not surprisingly, everyone has their favorite venue and maintains strongly held beliefs about the way crabs are supposed to be cooked and the spice blend that should be used for steaming. Needless to say, when Marylanders congregate for steamed crabs, its not unusual to overhear lively debate about who makes the best.

Having steamed crabs, at least for me, was always a festive occasion. Whether it was just the four of us (Mom, Dad, me and my Brother) around the kitchen table, a larger table set up on the driveway with invited friends, or an excursion to one of the local crab houses, I loved the way these dinners were staged. Brown paper rolled out to cover the table, wooden mallets for whacking and smashing the crabs, a roll of paper towels (it gets messy), bottomless pitchers of iced tea, an ice chest full of Natty Bo (National Bohemian Beer) for the adults, and a trash can next to the table was all you needed.

Dozens of steaming hot, heavily spiced crabs would be brought out on trays, then unceremoniously dumped onto the table. From this point forward, it was a bit of a free-for-all. We ate with our hands, spit pieces of shell back onto the table, and generally made a glorious mess of things until all of the crabs were gone. If you've never been to someone's home for steamed crabs, or have yet to attend an organized Maryland crab feast, make sure to put it on your bucket list.

My fondest memory of steamed crabs was at Gabler's - a no-frills crab house situated along the Bush River in Aberdeen Maryland - and a considerable drive from our suburban home. I'll never forget seeing the long, communally shared rows of picnic tables covered with brown kraft paper heaped with mound after mound of freshly seamed crabs. There must have been more than two hundred like-minded people cracking and hammering away at their crabs, all the while laughing, drinking, and spitting the night away.

While some of the more genteel diners would insist on a somewhat slower start to their meals, taking time to enjoy a bowl of crab soup or a crab cake platter, I walked in ready for the main event - the crabs. Even today, while I admit I enjoy a crab cake or three, I'm still insistent that the crabs come first. Just serve up the crab cakes along the way - a little bit of effortless crab indulgence to break up the wonderfully laborious job of cracking and picking at crabs.

Of course, a night of steamed crabs was never complete without dessert. Since my Mom was famous for her home baked cakes and pies, we would always have dessert at home. The best was peach pie with a big ol' scoop of vanilla ice cream on the side. Of course, her marble fudge bars and coffee cake were equally well received. That being said, and especially during the summer months when peaches were abundant, a freshly baked pie ruled the day.

Another equally memorable summertime treat was a fried chicken dinner at the Peter Pan Inn in the rural setting of Urbana, Maryland. As with Gabler's, Peter Pan represented a considerable drive into the boonies. From my youthful perspective, compared to the long walks to school that seemed to take forever, these drives into the far-reaching countryside filled with pastures and cornfields stretched on for an eternity (today, they've been plowed over and transformed into soulless housing developments and shopping centers).

To be completely honest, it was not the chicken that I enjoyed all that much. It was the apple butter paired with cottage cheese that was served as part of the salad course that I enjoyed the most. And of course, there were the corn fritters (hush puppies) that accompanied the chicken when the main course was served. While I am a huge fan of mashed potatoes and mac-n-cheese, freshly fried corn fritters generously dusted with confectioner's sugar are in the same league.

If you ever dined at Peter Pan, you know that the place was more than just the food. It was the long lines waiting for a table, the Southern-accented announcements over the loudspeaker calling your table, the hodge-podge of antiques, statues, and fountains that adorned the place inside and out, as well as the free-roaming peacocks that mingled with guests. And while I was too young to partake, there were the brightly colored, parasol adorned cocktails that were served in oversized hurricane glasses.

To say that a visit to Peter Pan was a sensory experience would be an understatement. Even the ride home with overstuffed and aching bellies was memorable.

In addition to these destination-oriented experiences, there were a number of culinary encounters that did not involve dining out. While too numerous to count, the most indelible were freshly pressed apple cider, coddies, and the ever-present supply of Stouffer's Welsh Rarebit that my Dad and I would enjoy for lunch and as midnight snacks.

Since I've mentioned how much I enjoyed the apple butter at Peter Pan, there was another place - Weber's Mill - that made the best damned apple butter around. I must admit that, while bringing home a few jars of that apple-licious spread was always something to look forward to, it was the old-fashioned cider press with its spinning wheels, slappety-slappety leather drive belts, and layers of crushed apples hidden behind a dripping wet, accordioned curtain that had my 6-year old imagination running wild. To this date, I have no idea how that amazing contraption worked but it was great fun watching everything in motion, listening to the cacophony of sounds, and taking in the heady aromas of freshly squeezed apples. Needless to say, a couple of bottles of cider always accompanied the apple butter that found its way into our shopping basket.

I've returned to Webber's as an adult, only to discover the quirky cider press that I marveled at in my youth has been replaced with a featureless, and undoubtedly more hygienic, stainless steel device kept far from peering eyes in a refrigerated processing room. While the cider and the butter are still good, the magic is missing.

I've since learned how to make apple butter for those rare occasions when I crave the sweet sensations of childhood. When I do, and while the apples are cooking, I'll close my eyes, inhale the fumes, and summon up those delicious memories.

Anyone who knows me well has learned that, given a choice between sweet and salty foods, I'll take the latter. So, while the apple butter from Webber's was good, the coddies that I'd buy from Wagner's Pharmacy, a small drug and convenience store in Pikesville not too far from where I lived, were even better. Typically consumed as a midday snack, and always between two saltine crackers with a slather of yellow mustard, coddies were a regular and inexpensive source of enjoyment.

If you've never seen or tasted a coddie, they used to be made from a mash of cooked cod and potato formed into small patties and deep fried until golden brown. Should you find them today, you'll probably find the fish has all but disappeared, leaving a sad, greasy affair that's nothing more than a somewhat spicy, fried potato cake. Unless I make them at home, I won't buy them anymore.

While my interest in all of these dishes were originally sparked by my Mom, there is one that I attribute to my Dad. While my Mom cooked from scratch using fresh and flavorful ingredients, all my Dad had to do is reach into the freezer and grab one of the many thin, red and black boxes that my Mom made sure were always in abundant supply.

Yes, my Dad was the master of frozen food, using the microwave and toaster with unparalleled dexterity to create his masterpiece - Stouffer's Welsh Rarebit. While it's hard to find today, every now and then you can find this stuff in the freezer aisle. Surprisingly, it's nearly as good as I remember.

For the uninitiated, Welsh Rarebit is a thick, cheesy sauce poured over slices of toasted bread. In some cases, and although it has no meat of any sort, this dish is frequently referred to as Welsh Rabbit. It is my understanding that, way back in the 18th century, there was a British hunter who returned home empty handed. With the cheese sauce and bread already prepared for the evening meal, everything continued as planned, sans bunny.

While I can no longer stomach industrialized and mass produced frozen foods, I've managed to piece together a wonderful version of this recipe that gives me tremendous pleasure - both for its incredible cheesiness as well as the way it brings back fond memories of time spent in the kitchen with my Dad.

# APPLE BUTTER
Makes about 6 cups

---

*INGREDIENTS*
1 1/2 cups apple juice concentrate
4 lbs. apples, peeled, cored, coarsely chopped
1/2 cup sugar
1/2 cup light brown sugar
1 teaspoon ground cinnamon
1/8 teaspoon allspice
1/8 teaspoon nutmeg

*DIRECTIONS*
In a large pot, bring the juice and apples to a boil, then reduce and simmer for 1 hour. Using an immersion blender, puree the cooked fruit until smooth. Add sugar, brown sugar, cinnamon, allspice and nutmeg and mix well.

Simmer uncovered for an additional one or two hours, stirring occasionally to prevent burning. Once a desired consistency is obtained, spoon into storage containers and refrigerate.

# CODDIES
Makes about 20

___

*INGREDIENTS*
1 1/2 lbs. cod
1/2 lb. potatoes, peeled, cut into large cubes
2 tablespoons milk
2 eggs, beaten
1 teaspoon onion powder
1/2 teaspoon mustard powder
1/2 teaspoon black pepper
1 teaspoon salt
1 teaspoon Worcestershire sauce
1/2 cup bread crumbs
Peanut oil, for frying

*DIRECTIONS*
Steam the cod until fully cooked. Transfer to a large bowl, break up thoroughly with a fork and allow to cool.

Cook the potatoes in boiling water until very tender. Drain completely, add milk, mash, then set aside and allow to cool.

In a large bowl, whisk together the egg, onion powder, mustard powder, pepper, salt, Worcestershire and bread crumbs. Add the fish and potatoes, then mix until thoroughly combined. Form into 1 1/2" balls and flatten slightly into patties.

Heat the oil in a large skillet until just below the smoking point. Cook the fish patties until browned on both sides. Transfer to a paper towel-covered plate and allow to drain.

When completely cooled, sandwich between two saltine crackers with a touch of yellow mustard.

# CORN FRITTERS
### Serves 4

---

*INGREDIENTS*
4 cups vegetable oil
1 cup flour, sifted
1 teaspoon baking powder
1 teaspoon granulated sugar
1/2 teaspoon salt
1 egg, lightly beaten
1/2 cup milk
1 tablespoon butter, melted
2 cups corn
confectioner's sugar, for dusting

*DIRECTIONS*
Heat oil in a heavy pot or deep fryer to 365°F.

To make the batter, combine the flour, baking powder, sugar and salt. Whisk in the egg, milk, and butter followed by the corn, making sure to mix everything thoroughly.

Drop the batter by teaspoons into the hot oil and fry until golden brown and crispy. Drain on paper towels.

Dust with confectioners sugar before serving.

Note: Check the temperature of the oil between batches, making sure it returns to 365 degrees.

# MARYLAND CRAB CAKES
Makes 6

---

*INGREDIENTS*

Crab Cake Spice Blend*

2 tablespoons celery salt

1 teaspoon dry mustard

1 teaspoon paprika

1/2 teaspoon bay leaf powder

1/4 teaspoon cinnamon

Crab Cakes

1 egg

3 tablespoons mayonnaise

1 tablespoon breadcrumbs

1 tablespoon parsley, finely chopped

2 teaspoons Crab Cake Spice Blend (see above)

1 lb. crab meat, lump backfin recommended

*DIRECTIONS*

Whisk together the egg, breadcrumbs, mayonnaise, parsley and Crab Cake Spice Blend. Using a spatula, gently fold in the crab meat, taking care not to break the lumps.

Divide the meat into 6 portions, forming each into a crab cake. Place on a baking sheet and broil for approximately 8 minutes. Once the first side is golden brown and toasted, carefully turn the cakes over and continue broiling for another 8 minutes, until fully browned.

Serve with tartar sauce and a wedge of lemon.

*If you don't want to make your own spice blend, simply use Old Bay, found in most supermarkets.

# MARYLAND CRAB DIP
## Serves 8

---

Great for summer entertaining. Serve this easy-to-make party favorite to special friends or anyone you want to impress.

*INGREDIENTS*
8 oz. cream cheese (softened)
1 lemon, juiced
1 tablespoon clam juice
1 tablespoon prepared horseradish
1/2 lb. fresh crab meat
salt and pepper to taste
(Optional: 2-3 dashes of Tabasco)
1 baguette, cut into 1/2" slices (or crackers), for dipping

*DIRECTIONS*
Place all ingredients (except crab) in bowl and mix thoroughly. Add crab and fold in gently, taking care not to unnecessarily break lumps of meat. Add salt and pepper to taste.

Pour into an oven-proof baking dish and bake uncovered at 375°F for 20-30 minutes until lightly browned and bubbly.

Serve while hot.

# MARBLED FUDGE BARS
Makes appx 48 bars

---

*INGREDIENTS*
<u>Chocolate Batter</u>
1 cup butter
8 oz. unsweetened chocolate
6 eggs
4 cups sugar
2 cups flour
1 teaspoon salt
2 teaspoons vanilla

<u>Vanilla Batter</u>
16 oz. cream cheese
2 eggs
1 cup sugar
2 teaspoons vanilla

*DIRECTIONS*
Grease a 13" x 18" x 1" sheet pan.

Preheat oven to 350°F.

Make the chocolate batter: In a double boiler (or a metal bowl placed over a pot of boiling water), melt and whisk together the butter and chocolate. As soon as these ingredients have melted, remove from heat.

In a large bowl, whisk the sugar and eggs together until fluffy. Add the chocolate mixture, followed by flour, salt and vanilla. Spread evenly in baking pan.

Make the vanilla batter: In another bowl, using a mixer, combine the cream cheese, sugar, egg, and vanilla.

Drop the vanilla mixture in dollops over the chocolate, leaving some space in between so the chocolate shows through.

Using a knife, lightly score the batter in a crisscross pattern to create a marbled effect.

Bake for 40 minutes or until a toothpick comes out clean.

Cool thoroughly before slicing into squares.

For immediate consumption, cover and store in the refrigerator. Alternatively, these bars can be wrapped in plastic wrap and frozen. They're actually quite enjoyable straight from the freezer.

---

*"Never eat more than you can lift"*
*Miss Piggy*

---

# WELSH RAREBIT
Serves 2 for dinner, 4 for appetizers

*INGREDIENTS*
2 tablespoons butter
1 tablespoon flour
1/2 cup light ale
1/4 cup milk
3/4 lb. extra sharp Cheddar, shredded
2 teaspoons Worcestershire sauce
1/2 teaspoon dry mustard
dash Tabasco
2 egg yolks
6 slices bread, toasted, cut into 1-inch squares
Black pepper, to taste

*DIRECTIONS*
Melt butter in the bottom of a medium saucepan. Whisk in the flour to make a roux, followed by the ale and milk.

Gradually whisk in the cheese, followed by the Worcestershire, mustard, Tabasco and egg yolks.

To serve, place equal amounts of toasted bread squares on each plate. Pour the sauce over top, then garnish with black pepper.

 Not only did I enjoy this elixir in polite company without making twisted faces and shivering all over when swallowed, I discovered the flavorful nuance that tequila had to offer.

**A**lthough I had enjoyed a variety of life altering experiences at home, including a family vacation across the United States as well as a few weeks in the Caribbean visiting Puerto Rico, Trinidad, St, Thomas, and Martinique, I was undeniably naïve when it came to the ways of the world. I imagine this was due, in part, to the fact that I grew up as the shunned, ignored, and somewhat ostracized "fat kid" in the neighborhood. In addition, while my parents believed strongly in education, were politically liberal, and undeniably loving, they were very straight laced when it came to matters of style and popular culture. There was virtually no music in the house, alcohol was rarely consumed, and the idea of engaging in athletics and outdoor activities of any sort was inconceivable.

In school, it was no surprise that I was completely inept when it came to matters of sports, trending fashions, and popular music and was both shy and awkward around girls. While my talents in art were recognized and encouraged at home as well as in school, it did nothing for me socially, especially when the topics of discussion were completely unrelated. When you consider how insensitive children can be, I was understandably teased, belittled, and insulted - finding myself relegated to the realm of nerds, geeks, misfits and oddballs.

Needless to say, upon graduation from high school, I was hardly prepared to enter the world as a fully functional individual, let alone manage my affairs in an intelligent and adult-like manner. This being said, the rule in our household was that, after high school, you went to college. Accordingly, and right on schedule at the ripe old age of 17, I was sent off to Tucson to attend the University of Arizona.

As a matter of introduction, I arrived in Tucson in 1973. With its population hovering around 300,000, it had all the trappings of a small desert town. Franchised fast food was limited to a few operators, high-end restaurants were equally sparse, there was no Food TV (cable TV was still emerging, available in just a few larger markets), and the only reason anyone cared about food was primarily because they were hungry.

Considering that my deeper interest in food, and the culinary training I pursued, would not begin for another 15 years, the foods I preferred during my Freshman year were pretty much limited to what was available in the Student Union cafeteria or nearby restaurants. Pizza, hot dogs, hamburgers, soft serve ice cream, and beer (of course) were dietary mainstays.

I started discovering new foods quite by accident, starting with the occasional Friday night encounters with my Mom's Tucson-based cousin Sid. With a wife and four kids, he would moonlight on weekends in a liquor store to make ends meet. Every now and then on a Friday or Saturday night, I would keep him company for the last few hours of his shift, listening to time-worn stories about his adventures in the Army or the inside scoop about some of the people on my Mom's side of the family that I had either never met or barely knew.

Once the shop was tidied up, the register closed out, and the doors locked, we would head out for what Sid referred to as "Coffee and..." We never went anywhere fancy - just one of the late night or all-night coffee shops in the area.

Since the concept of "Coffee and..." was new to me, and I really did not know my way around a coffee shop menu, Sid always had recommendations. While a typical order would be "Coffee and... eggs," the most memorable were "Coffee and... pecan pie" or, better still, "Coffee and... biscuits and gravy."

If you knew my Mom, you know her pies were second to none. My favorite was peach, followed closely by strawberry rhubarb. Since she also made blueberry, sour cherry, apple, and pumpkin, I never believed I was missing out... until Sid introduced me to "Coffee and... pecan pie.

My life was irreversibly changed. I fell head over heels in love with this sweet, dense, and incredibly satisfying slice of heaven. Having subsequently learned that my Mom did not care for this particular variety of pie (hence never having it at home), it was clear that I would have to learn how to make this uber-rich dessert for myself.

The other life altering coffee shop encounter shared with Sid was "Coffee and... biscuits & gravy." I still remember

Sid's surprise when I revealed this was something I had never tasted. I must admit that, after I had "Coffee and... biscuits & gravy" for the first time, it would become a regular order every time we'd get together.

After decades of biscuits & gravy from restaurants wherever I've lived or visited, I decided to learn how to make this dish at home. While I have come up with a reasonable recipe, the variations found at greasy spoons and faded diners and are far better than anything I can make at home.

Should you happen to be in the vicinity, some of my favorite destinations for biscuits & gravy have included Ashland Cafe (Cockeysville, MD), Rae's Restaurant (Santa Monica, CA), Tastee Diner (Bethesda, MD), and Metro Diner (Jacksonville Beach, FL).

Back in the 70s, Mexican food had not yet gained nationwide popularity. It was virtually unknown outside of the American southwest, making it impossible for this clueless gringo from Baltimore to have any idea what Mexican food looked, smelled, or tasted like.

With its proximity to the Mexican border, there was a sizable Latino population in Tucson and throughout Arizona. Needless to say, ingredients for Mexican foods were abundant in local supermarkets and there were plenty of Mexican restaurants scattered around town.

I still remember one of my first visits to the Student Union cafeteria, discovering that a significant portion of the serving line was dedicated to Mexican food. The menu listed strange and peculiarly named dishes that included tacos, burritos, chimichangas, quesadillas, and tostadas. Adding to my confusion were exotic and never before encountered ingredients that included guacamole, salsa, refried beans, tortillas, and queso blanco. I might as well have landed on another planet, finding myself lacking the vocabulary and experience to order from the menu.

Over time, I made it my job to sample everything, developing a preference for tacos and burritos. And while my life-long preference for cheese-based dishes was not yet fully formed, I was leaning towards cheesy quesadillas. Nowadays, I make many of these dishes at home and thoroughly enjoy the occasional visit to truly ethnic Mexican restaurants, especially those in Arizona and New Mexico.

In keeping with the Mexican theme, having reached the legal drinking age of 19 while living in Arizona, one of my more important discoveries was tequila. While everyone on campus was extolling the virtues of Mezcal and the hallucinogenic quality of the worm at the bottom of the bottle, a friend of the family introduced me to Sauza Conmemorativo Añejo. This was an undeniably better class of tequila, one that could be sipped at a leisurely pace.

Not only could I enjoy this elixir in polite company without making twisted faces and shivering all over when swallowed, it allowed me to discover the flavorful nuance that tequila has to offer.

When not sipping Conmemorativo (it was too expensive for me on a student's budget), the default tequila-based cocktail quickly became the margarita. It didn't matter much if it was on the rocks, with or without a salted rim, frozen or fruity, I drank them all with abandon.

Of course, being new to the idea of cocktails, my friends and I did not limit ourselves to margaritas alone. We were equal opportunity drinkers, throwing back Tequila Sunrises, Harvey Wallbangers, Whiskey Sours, 7 & 7s, Screwdrivers, Greyhounds, Black Russians and Long Island Iced Teas with reckless abandon. If it was sweet enough to drink without really tasting the alcohol, we would indulge.

It goes without saying, the degree I received from the University of Arizona in Graphic Design has been undeniably valuable. This being said, the education I obtained from Arizona's countless and colorful watering holes, including the Cushing Street Bar, Solarium, Gentle Ben's, Green Dolphin, Bum Steer, Jekyll & Hyde's, and Jim's Place (Where Elite Meat Meet Meat), have contributed significantly to the way I entered adulthood. While they did not issue diplomas, I successfully learned about dating, mixology, hospitality, drug and alcohol abuse, music, swing dancing, lip reading, tobacco, fashion, body language, sex, casual dining, darts, and pool.

Keeping this in mind, there was one particular Friday afternoon after a long week of classes when my culinary education took a memorable leap forward. Although Fridays were usually earmarked for beers and pizza at The Last Chance Pizza Mill (the place known for deep dish pizza and cheap beer), a group of friends suggested we check out the 2-for-1 happy hour special at a bar on the other side of campus.

Over a span of a couple of hours, we became a well muddled, excessively giggly, visibly unsteady, and openly boisterous group whose deportment contrasted sharply to that of the bar's predominantly mature patrons. Let's just say they did not partake in happy hour with the same degree of ardor, relish, or enthusiasm as we did. Sensing we were having far too much fun to hang with a bunch of stick-in-the-mud old farts, it was decided, and I imagine hotel management breathed a sigh of relief, that we should move the party to someone's home.

Seeing that Nancy (one of our group) was willing to have us descend upon her place, and had not participated in happy hour with the same degree of gusto and thirst as the rest of us, we safely piled into her car, picked up some munchies along the way, and headed over to her place. Upon arrival, we gracelessly distributed ourselves across whatever space we could find in chairs, on the couch, or across the floor.

Nancy, being the ultimate host, offered us drinks along with an assortment of chips to settle us in. Once served, she headed off to the kitchen to cook. Recognizing the kitchen as the most desirable place to congregate, a few of us kept her company. When I asked what she was making, I learned that, in addition to the beer and chips picked up on the way home, she had also purchased a pair of artichokes.

The key to this story is twofold. The first is remembering that I was in an exceptionally robust state of intoxication. Secondly, and up to this point in my coming of age, I had never seen an artichoke, witnessed its preparation, or eaten one.

What amazed me was how excited everyone appeared to be about the arrival of the cooked 'chokes. Without hesitation, people were pulling off leaves, dipping them in butter, and nibbling on their edges. It didn't matter how good the butter was for dipping. I simply found the whole process, and the vegetable itself, a tedious and unsatisfying waste of time. It wasn't until all of the leaves had been consumed that I was called over once again. Nancy introduced me to the artichoke heart, explained that I could eat the whole thing, and suggested I try once again.

Thinking I was being played for the drunken fool that I was, I took a reluctant bite. While it took longer than usual for the sensation to register, the artichoke heart was actually good. Creamy texture. Delicate flavor. How this leafy globe was magically transformed into something so truly remarkable was, for my befuddled brain, the ninth wonder of the world.

I must admit that, even today, I don't care much for grazing on artichoke leaves. But when the opportunity comes along to enjoy artichoke hearts, I'm always at the front of the line. And I always remember Nancy for making the introduction.

# ARTICHOKE DIP
### Serves 8

---

*INGREDIENTS*

2 (14oz.) cans artichoke hearts, chopped

7 oz. green chilies (canned)

1 cup Parmesan, grated

1/2 cup mayonnaise

1 teaspoon sweet paprika

pinch cayenne

1 baguette, sliced into 1/2-inch slices

*DIRECTIONS*

In a large bowl, mix together the artichokes, chilies, Parmesan, mayonnaise, paprika and cayenne. Transfer the mixture to an oven-proof baking dish. Bake uncovered for 25 minutes until slightly browned and bubbly.

Serve straight from the oven with plenty of sliced baguette for dipping.

# BUTTERMILK BISCUITS
Makes 20 biscuits

---

*INGREDIENTS*
2 cups flour
1 teaspoon baking powder
1/2 teaspoon baking soda
1/2 teaspoon salt
1/2 cup butter (cold, cut into small pieces)
3/4 cup buttermilk

*DIRECTIONS*
Preheat the oven to 450°F.

Place the flour, baking powder, baking soda and salt together in a food processor. Pulse in the butter, a little bit at a time, until the flour becomes crumbly. Slowly add the buttermilk to form a dough. If the dough is wet, add a bit more flour.

Roll the dough on a floured board to a 1/2 inch thickness. Using a 2 1/2-inch cookie cutter, cut into individual rounds.

Place the rounds on a baking sheet, then into the oven for 15-20 minutes until lightly browned.

Serve warm from the oven or cool on a rack for later use.

# GUACAMOLE
## Serves 8

---

*INGREDIENTS*
1/2 cup ripe tomatoes, finely diced
1/3 cup red onion, finely diced
2 tablespoons lime juice
1 tablespoon cilantro, chopped
1/2 teaspoon garlic, minced
1/2 teaspoon salt
1/2 teaspoon cumin
4 ripe avocados
Tabasco, to taste

*DIRECTIONS*
In a large bowl, mix together the tomatoes, onion, cilantro, lime juice, garlic, salt, and cumin.

Cut the avocados in half, remove the seed, scoop out the flesh and add to the mixture. Using a fork, mash the avocado and mix thoroughly.

Add Tabasco, additional salt and/or lime juice, to taste.

Refrigerate for 2 to 4 hours. Check and adjust seasoning, as needed, before serving.

# PEACH MARGARITA
### Serves 4

---

*INGREDIENTS*
4 oz. Añejo tequila
2 oz. peach schnapps
1 tablespoon sugar
2 cups fresh peaches, coarsely diced, frozen*
3 cups crushed ice
cold water, as needed

*DIRECTIONS*
Pour the tequila, schnapps and sugar into the blender. Add the frozen peaches and ice and blend at high speed until a nice slush is created. Add cold water, as needed, to achieve the desired consistency.

Optional: You may wish to rim the glasses with sugar. If so, run a wedge of lime around the lip of the glass to moisten, then dip the rim into a plate of sugar. If you want to make a more colorful presentation, use yellow or orange sanding sugars,** or a colorful mixture of both.

*Freezing the peaches in advance makes for a thicker and substantially colder margarita.

**Sanding (decorative) sugars are available in the baking aisle of most supermarkets.

# FRESH PEACH SALSA
## Serves 8

A delicious alternative to tomato salsa. The key to success is sweet, ripe fruit.

*INGREDIENTS*
4 ripe peaches, peeled and coarsely chopped
1 small red onion, finely chopped
1 red capsicum, finely chopped
1/4 cup fresh mint, finely chopped
2 birdseye chilies, finely chopped
1 lime, juiced
1 tablespoon sugar
salt and pepper, to taste

*DIRECTIONS*
Prepare all of the ingredients, then mix together in a large bowl. Cover and refrigerate overnight, mixing the ingredients once or twice. Letting this dish marinate overnight allows the ingredients and flavors to blend. Taste before serving, adding extra lime juice, sugar and/or mint to taste.

NOTE: This recipe is equally delicious with mangoes. I prefer the golden champagne variety.

# PECAN PIE
## Serves 8

___

*INGREDIENTS*

Pie Crust

1/2 cup less 1 tablespoon shortening (Crisco)

3 tablespoons boiling water

1 teaspoon milk

1/2 teaspoon salt

1 1/4 cups flour, sifted

Filling

3 eggs

1 cup sugar

1/2 teaspoon salt

2 tablespoons butter

1/2 cup dark corn syrup

1/2 cup whipping cream

1 tablespoon vanilla

1/4 cup brandy

1 cup pecan halves

*DIRECTIONS*

To make the crust: Place the shortening in a large bowl along with the boiling water and milk. Using a fork, cut and mix the ingredients until most of the liquid has been absorbed. Add the flour and salt, mixing together until you can form a ball of dough.

Roll out the dough on a floured surface to a size that will fit in the bottom of a 9" pie plate, allowing about a 1/2" of dough extra all around. Place the rolled crust into the pie plate, folding the extra dough under the rim to make an edge. Crimp the rolled edge with the tip of a fork.

Preheat the oven to 375° F.

To make the filling, beat together the eggs, sugar, salt, butter, corn syrup, cream, vanilla, brandy in a large bowl, followed by the pecans.

Pour the filling into the crust and bake for approximately 40 minutes, or until set. Cool before serving.

Serve with vanilla ice cream, whipped cream, or both!

---

*"There is no love sincerer than*
*the love of food."*
*George Bernard Shaw*

---

# QUESADILLA WITH GARLIC SHRIMP
### Serves 4 - 6

*INGREDIENTS*
1 tablespoon olive oil
1 teaspoon garlic
1 lb. shrimp (21-25 count), peeled and cleaned
4 flour tortillas, large (for burritos)
8 oz. extra sharp cheddar, grated
8 oz. Monterrey Jack, grated
4 oz (1 can) green chilies, chopped
1/4 cup cilantro, chopped

*DIRECTIONS*
Pour the oil into a pan over medium high heat. Add the garlic and sauté for 1 minute. Add the shrimp, cooking on one side for 1 1/2 minutes, then turned and cooked on the other side for 1 1/2 minutes more. When done, remove from the heat. Cut each shrimp in half lengthwise and set aside.

To make the quesadillas, use a large pan over medium heat. Place one tortilla in the pan, sprinkle a quarter of both cheeses evenly over top, followed by a quarter of the shrimp along with a sprinkling of green chilies and cilantro. Once the cheeses have melted and the underside is browned, fold the quesadilla in half, then transfer to a cutting board and cut into four wedges using a pizza wheel or chef's knife.

Repeat this process until all four quesadillas are fully cooked and sliced. Arrange the quesadilla wedges on one large serving platter or individual plates. Garnish with a squeeze of fresh lime, salsa, guacamole, and/or sour cream.

# SAUSAGE GRAVY
Makes about 4 cups

---

*INGREDIENTS*

1 lb. breakfast sausage, casings removed
3 tablespoons butter
3 tablespoons flour
2 cups milk
pinch cayenne
salt and pepper, to taste

*DIRECTIONS*

Cook the sausage in a medium saucepan, breaking up any clumps that may occur. Once fully browned, use a slotted spoon to transfer the sausage to a bowl and set aside.

Using the same saucepan, add the butter. When fully melted, whisk in the flour to make a roux. Slowly whisk in the milk, followed by the sausage, cayenne, salt and pepper. Continue cooking until the gravy is smooth and thick.

Serve over freshly baked buttermilk biscuits.

# TOMATO SALSA
### Serves 8

---

## INGREDIENTS
5 cups ripe tomatoes, diced
1/2 cup red onion, finely chopped
1/4 cup cilantro, finely chopped
1 Jalapeño pepper, seeded, finely chopped
3 tablespoons tomato paste
1 tablespoon lime juice
1 teaspoon sugar
1/2 teaspoon salt
1/4 teaspoon black pepper

## DIRECTIONS
In a large bowl, mix together the tomatoes, onion, cilantro, Jalapeño, tomato paste, lime juice, sugar, salt, and pepper. Cover and chill for 4 hours or overnight.

After 4 hours, stir and taste the salsa. Add lime juice, sugar or salt, to taste. Check and adjust the flavors once again, just before serving.

 There were vendors on every street grilling up aromatic coils of Italian sausage and caramelizing tantalizing mounds of onions and peppers. Like a hungry dog, I would stop at every stall to get a proper look.

**G**rowing up in Baltimore meant easy access to New York. Whether my parents loaded us into the Country Squire wagon for family excursions, teachers herded us into yellow school buses for field trips, or I simply caught a train into town to take in the sights, sounds, and flavors of the "big smoke," adventures into Manhattan have been frequent, engaging, eye opening, educational, and undeniably delicious. Even today, and no matter where I wander, there is always something (or someone) just ahead that catches my attention, stimulates my senses, and delights my imagination.

When it comes to close encounters of a culinary kind, my earliest memory takes place at Mamma Leone's. At that time, and in operation since 1906, it was one of New York's largest and most celebrated Italian restaurants. Operating in the heart of the city's theatre district, this Italian landmark had been enticing patrons, including American presidents and Hollywood celebrities, with meals of gluttonous proportion for years.

My memory of Mamma Leone's, however, starts in an average sized dining room dimly lit by strings of small white lights hanging from the ceiling and zig zagging across the space from wall to wall. While I am not entirely sure, I seem to believe additional light came from candles that had been wedged into empty, straw-wrapped Chianti bottles and placed on all the tables.

With absolutely no recall of the meal itself, other than being seated at a sizable table with my Mom, Dad, and brother Rick, I must conclude that the impression made by the spaghetti, veal, or lasagna must have been standard fare - similar to many other Italian meals we regularly enjoyed at Sabatino's in Baltimore's renowned Little Italy. What is indelibly etched into my consciousness, however, is the waiter presenting a sizable plate of wonderfully thin and crispy strips of fried pastry generously sprinkled with confectioner's sugar. Apparently, this sweet treat was a house specialty served to everyone at the conclusion of their meal.

While I could not find a menu that described what these were, research indicates they are a traditional Italian sweet that Mamma Leone's called sfrappole. I've also learned that, depending on where you encounter these crispy confections in Italy, they may also be called Crostoli, Chiacchiere, Frappe, Bugie, Cenci, or Galani and are typically served during Carnevale (Mardi Gras).

For me, this eatery's undeniably festive setting, combined with the arrival of those remarkably light and delicately crunchy fritters, is one of my fondest memories of Manhattan.

There is no doubt that Italians know how to eat. Should you have any doubt, and since Mamma Leone's closed in 1987, then wander into New York's historic Little Italy during the Feast of San Gennaro. No matter when you read these words, I'm sure this autumnal street festival, now approaching 100 years of operation, will still be taking place. Celebrating the Patron Saint of Naples, the Feast of San Gennaro keeps the spirit of New York's early Italian immigrants alive through colorful parades, lively music, and an endless stream of heavenly sweet and savory Italian treats.

My memory of the Feast is based on a family visit to New York when I was just knee high to a grasshopper. Continuously distracted by the lively festivities, invigorating music, and tantalizing aromas, and on the verge of sensory overload, I was constantly trailing behind my parents as we walked between Mulberry, Grand, and Hester streets.

The fact that I was a wee lad meant that taking in many of the sights and sounds along the way was a bit of a challenge. Surrounded by adults twice my height, everything that attracted my attention was taking place just beyond my ability to see, forcing me to appreciate things on tippy-toes and in small glimpses as breaks in the crowds would open, or from the occasional elevated vantage point whenever I could find a box or ledge to stand on.

I'm telling you this because, much to my delight, there were vendor stalls on every street grilling up aromatic coils of Italian sausage and caramelizing tantalizing mounds of onions and peppers. While my parents kept on walking, and like a hungry dog that has escaped its leash, I would stop at every stall to get a proper look and gaze longingly at these sizzling delights.

I don't believe I had ever tasted an Italian sausage before this day (yes, my parents finally acquiesced). Ever since, I have become quite the aficionado of these pork, fennel and spice infused treats, finding ways to enjoy Italian sausage on pasta, in sauces and stews, and of course, on a freshly baked Italian bread roll topped with "the works" whenever possible.

I always look forward to visiting with the food vendors that park themselves on street corners throughout the city. No matter the time of day, and assuming Italian sausages are on the menu, I am regularly compelled to stop and enjoy one of these ethnic wonders... loaded with onions and peppers of course. And if they don't have Italian sausage, there is my next favorite version of tube steak - the delectable, red hot, all-American, take-me-out-to-the-ballgame, hot diggety dog.

It goes without saying that I learned to like hot dogs well before my first visit to New York. Since the idea of grabbing a dog from a corner vendor is not something that's available in the sheltered suburbs of Baltimore, my Mom would boil, pan fry, or grill a few dogs and serve them to us on a toasted roll with mustard and pickle relish. When she made hot dogs for my Dad, she was sure to include a couple of slices of pan-fried bologna.

With an insatiable appetite for all things "sausage," no trip to New York is complete without patronizing the city's ubiquitous hot dog vendors. It's important to note that, over time, I have learned to distinguish between hot dog brands and will only patronize carts proudly serving either Hebrew National, Sabrett or Nathan dogs. While Hebrew National are my favorite, I will happily scarf down any dog bearing one of these three names without the slightest hesitation.

There is no limit to my fascination with hot dogs. While my

standard dog is modestly adorned with mustard, variations including grilled onions, sauerkraut, grated cheese, chili con carne, sweet pickle relish, spicy brown mustard, and even ketchup are always welcomed. Of course, there is no humanly way to walk and eat these piled-high creations without spilling them onto shoes, pants and shirt. Even if it's just mustard, and believing I have taken great care, I'll look down to find a brightly hued splat somewhere on my outfit.

When I am on the move, especially in New York, I've found it prudent to order my dogs plain, effectively avoiding potentially embarrassing spills. In this regard, flaking breadcrumbs are the worst offenders and no big deal. After all, they can be easily brushed away and will be eagerly enjoyed by the city's diverse population of winged and four-legged urban wildlife.

Ultimately, and no matter the situation or time of day, there is always sufficient room in my stomach for hot dogs.

As an art student craving new ideas, taking the train from Baltimore into New York was frequent, especially during holidays. Not only would I satisfy my cravings for creative stimulation, there would inevitably be a place discovered, meal consumed, or beverage imbibed that would provide some of my most enjoyable and enduring memories.

From a culinary perspective, this included regular visits to a tiny hole-in-the-wall bagel shop in Penn Station. As soon as the train would arrive, I'd make a beeline to this oasis of freshly baked bagels - wasting no time ordering a dark, dense, and slightly sweet pumpernickel bagel slathered with a thick layer of cream cheese and salty lox (smoked salmon). With this sandwich-sized feast in hand, I was suitably primed for all of the sensational events that would follow throughout the day.

As with so many other retailers in Penn Station, this little slice of heaven has been replaced by a tacky outlet for cheap post-cards and trashy tourist memorabilia. Since I take the train into New York at least once a year, I acknowledge my arrival with fond memories of bagels, lox and cream cheese.

While culinary crawls through the various ethnic neighborhoods of New York including Chinatown, Koreatown, and Little Italy are undeniably exciting - sampling new, unusual, and unfamiliar dishes along the way - nothing embodies the flavor of the Big Apple better than a multi-layered corned beef or pastrami sandwich with coleslaw, Russian dressing, chopped liver, and Swiss cheese. And while I know everyone has their preferences, the best of the best in terms of gastronomic beauty and overall culinary performance came from either the Carnegie Deli (sadly, this iconic purveyor of corned beef and pastrami closed a few years ago) and Katz's Delicatessen (still operating on Houston Street in the Lower East Side). In my humble opinion, no visit to New York is complete without one of these monstrous and artfully stratified constructions.

I still travel to New York on a regular basis, usually to attend the Summer Fancy Food Show and enjoy a hot dog or two. Recognizing there are always exciting culinary discoveries to be made, innovative new restaurants to visit, and inspired cu-linary creations to be tasted, setting aside time for a culinary crawl and a few enjoyable hours of adventurous grazing is always on my agenda. No matter where I end up, tasty treats are always available just down the street, around the corner, and a few steps away.

# MOM'S CHOPPED LIVER
## Serves 8 - 10

*INGREDIENTS*
1 lb. chicken livers, drained
2 eggs, whole (do not crack)
1 small onion
1 tablespoon chicken fat*
1 teaspoon salt
1/2 teaspoon black pepper

*DIRECTIONS*
Fill a large saucepan halfway with cold water and place over high heat. Add the livers and whole eggs and bring to a boil. Reduce heat to a slow boil and cook for 15 minutes. The livers will be fully cooked and eggs hard-boiled. Drain, peel the eggs, and set everything aside to cool.

Using a meat grinder (you can also use a food processor for a smoother consistency), grind the livers, eggs and onions. Add the chicken fat, salt and pepper and mix thoroughly.

Add additional salt & pepper to taste.

Refrigerate at least 1 hour before serving.

*Chicken fat, also known as schmaltz or shmalz, can be found in kosher markets.

# COLESLAW
## Serves 12

---

*INGREDIENTS*
1 head cabbage, thinly sliced
1 onion, thinly sliced
1 green pepper, thinly sliced
1 cup vinegar
3/4 cup peanut oil
1 tablespoon salt
1 tablespoon celery seed
1 teaspoon dry mustard
3/4 cup sugar

*DIRECTIONS*
Using a food processor with a thin slicing blade, shred the cabbage, onion, and green pepper. When finished, transfer all of the vegetables to a large mixing bowl.

Combine the vinegar, oil, salt, celery seed and dry mustard in a saucepan and bring to a boil. Remove from heat, add the sugar and stir until completely dissolved. Pour the mixture over the sliced vegetables and toss. Place the coleslaw in the refrigerator and marinate overnight. Toss before serving.

Slaw will keep up to two weeks in the refrigerator.

# PENN STATION POTATOES
*Makes 24 pieces*

---

While not the same as the wonderful pumpernickel bagels with lox and cream cheese that I enjoyed on my visits to New York, these tasty little treats pay flavorful homage.

*INGREDIENTS*
12 red potatoes, small (not larger than a golf ball)
1/2 cup cream cheese, softened
1/2 cup sour cream
4 oz. smoked salmon (lox)
2 tablespoons red onion, finely chopped
2 tablespoons caraway seeds
2 tablespoons lemon zest

*DIRECTIONS*
Place the potatoes in a large pot with enough cold water to more than cover. Bring to a boil over medium high heat and cook for approximately 20 minutes, until potatoes are tender. Transfer to a colander, rinse with cold water, then set aside to drain and cool.

Once the potatoes are cooled, slice a very thin piece from each end (allowing them to stand up on their own), then cut the potatoes in half. Using a small spoon, scoop out a small amount from the center of each potato half.

To make the filling, whisk together the cream cheese and sour cream. Using a decorator bag, pipe equal amounts of filling into each of the scooped out potato halves. Sprinkle a small amount of red onion and caraway seeds over top.

Cut the salmon into 2-inch x 4-inch strips, roll up each strip and cut crosswise into 4 pieces. Place the rolled salmon on top of the filling. Using a tweezer, place a few strands of lemon zest on top of the salmon.

Arrange the fully assembled potatoes on a large tray and serve.

Best served at room temperature.

―――――――――――――――

*"All you need is love. But a little chocolate now and then doesn't hurt."*
*Charles M. Schultz*

―――――――――――――――

# SFRAPPOLE
Makes about 72 pieces

---

*INGREDIENTS*

2 eggs
4 tablespoons sugar
2 tablespoons apple cider vinegar
1 teaspoon lemon zest
1/2 teaspoon vanilla extract
1/8 teaspoon salt
2 tablespoons butter, melted
2 1/4 cups flour, more for rolling out dough
vegetable oil, for deep frying
1 cup powdered sugar, for dusting

*DIRECTIONS*

In a large bowl, whisk together the eggs, sugar, cider vinegar, lemon zest, vanilla and salt, adding the butter last. Mix in the flour, a little at a time, until a dough is formed that is no longer sticky. Knead the dough on a floured surface for about 5 minutes, then wrap with plastic. Place the dough in the refrigerator and allow to rest for about 15 minutes.

Divide the dough into two balls. Wrap one in plastic and return to the refrigerator while you roll out the other.

Roll the dough on a floured surface, making it as thin as possible. Using a pastry wheel, cut the dough into thin strips approximately 1 inch wide and 3 inches long.

Heat the oil in a deep fryer to 375°F. When hot, drop a few dough strips into the oil, making sure to separate them while cooking. The strips will float on the surface of the oil. After about 1 minute and they begin to brown, flip them over. Once lightly browned on both sides, transfer the strips to a rack to drain and cool.

Continue rolling and cooking the remaining dough. When all of the dough is cooked and completely cooled, dust with confectioner's sugar and serve.

NOTE: Goes great with a bowl of sorbet, ice cream, cup of hot chocolate or cappuccino.

---

*"Ask not what you can do for your country. Ask what's for lunch."*
*Orson Welles*

---

I ordered a ham and gruyere crepe. To my delight, it was hot, gooey, rich and cheesy, displaying a wonderfully soft texture. It was, second only to hot dogs.

Paris was the first of several European cities I visited as part of a backpacking adventure that took place in the summer of 1977, immediately following my graduation from the University of Arizona and before I moved to Los Angeles to launch a career in graphic design. At that time, setting aside a few weeks, or even months, to traverse the world was what any self-respecting graduate did before becoming a contributing member of the American workforce.

While resources were limited (I didn't make a lot of money working at part-time college jobs), airfares were relatively inexpensive and Arthur Frommer's "Europe on $5 a Day" was the oft-followed doctrine for affordable youthful adventures. Unfortunately, the book was originally published in 1957, intended for American GI's traveling around Europe, and a meal consisting of roast veal, stuffing, carrots and potatoes for as little as 42 cents (as described in the first edition) was no longer a reality. For me, there was no way that I would enjoy my travels if limited to a meager $5.00 a day.

Fortunately, "Europe on $10 a Day" was published in 1975, just in time for me to buy a Eurail Pass, stitch a Grateful Dead "skull and roses" patch onto my backpack, clean my Swiss Army knife (making sure the toothpick and tweezers were in place), and head off to the airport for adventures across the Atlantic.

It's important to note that, while I've always enjoyed good food, my passion for all things edible had not yet been developed. Additionally, I possessed limited social skills, was a long-haired wannabe hippie, incredibly naive, and had never been overseas on my own. When it came to foreign languages, I was limited to a tourist's vocabulary in Spanish - most importantly "Quiero mas tequila por favor" and "Donde esta el cuarto de baño?" It goes without saying - I really didn't have much to work with.

Keeping in mind that ATM's had not yet been invented, credit cards were not widely accepted, and every country had its own currency, my first order of business upon arrival in Paris was exchanging a few of my traveler's checks ("Don't leave home without them.") for French francs. What I failed to understand, and more importantly anticipate, was that the majority of businesses throughout Europe, including banks, closed early on Saturday and remained closed throughout the day on Sunday. Since I arrived on a Sunday, I found myself virtually penniless, stranded at the train station, unable to speak the language, and had absolutely no idea where I was going.

It seemed the only retailer open for business inside the train station was a newsstand. Realizing this would be my best hope, I approached the sales lady to see if she would exchange my traveler's checks. With just one look, it was clear she took me for just another ignorant, long-haired American backpacker without a scrap of sense regarding travel in Europe.

With an audible snort, she admonished me to never arrive in a foreign country without having local currency. She also told me I would be able to find an open exchange catering to tourists in the city center. To my surprise, she took pity - giving me just enough money to purchase a Metro ticket that would get me into town. With my newfound good fortune, explicit directions, and an agenda, I sheepishly expressed my thanks and went on my way.

Before I embarked on this European adventure, one of my college buddies indicated he would be traveling Europe around the same time and suggested we met up in France. Realizing we were arriving from different airports and did not know who would reach Paris first, we agreed to meet on the Left Bank near the Notre-Dame Cathedral - hanging out for the day until we connected.

Our planning, to say the least, was ill-conceived. Even if we had both been in the same place at the same time, it was doubtful we would have spotted each other among the throngs of Parisians going about their daily business and wide-eyed tourists taking in the sights. Talk about finding a needle in a haystack. Sheesh!

Of course, if we had cell phones, things would have been completely different. Between text messaging and Google maps, we would have connected in a second. Considering this was the summer of '77, and the most advanced handheld technology available at that time was either a Texas Instruments calculator (standard issue in collegiate science classes) or Star

Fleet communicator (standard issue on the U.S.S. Enterprise), it was no surprise that we never connected.

Realizing that the day was more than half over, the rendezvous was a failure, and I would be left to my own devices, the time had come to make some quick decisions. With the help of my handy-dandy "Europe on $10 a Day," and before the sun went down, I managed to obtain local currency, purchase a map of the city, find basic accommodations at a local hostel, and safely hunker down for the evening.

I woke with the rising sun, refreshed but understandably anxious about how I would start my exploration of the city. In spite of the previous day's dramas and absence of advance planning, I quickly dressed, grabbed my map, and headed out to the streets. I figured that, as long as I had gotten this far, I might as well get out there and see what in the City of Lights had to offer.

Without an itinerary or pre-conceived set of expectations, I set off to discover Paris - meandering down the many cobble-stone laneways that laced their way through the city. Before I had gone more than a couple of blocks, I found myself staring into the window of a patisserie overflowing with fanciful pastries unlike any I had ever seen. Brightly colored cakes covered with fondant and decorative icing, unusually shaped cookies festooned with nonpareils, and tarts glistening with glazed fruit. Without a doubt, I was transfixed... and drooling.

As I considered these sweet delights, a voice from behind said "You don't want any of those. They're too fattening." When I turned, I was greeted by the smiling face of a middle-aged American man who introduced himself as Sheldon. As we spoke, and after I confessed that I had just arrived and absolutely no idea where I was heading, Sheldon mentioned that he knew his way around town and would be delighted to have my company for the next few hours.

Without fully understanding the situation, Sheldon whisked me off to Montemartre and the open air art market just below the Basilica Sacre-Coeur. This was the setting for my first European style espresso accompanied by a French baguette filled with ham and brie. While I was still craving some of the sweets from the patisserie, my initiation into Parisian culinary culture was well and truly underway.

Along with the introduction to Parisian street food, this was also the first time (but not the last) that I encountered an enthusiastic advance from a man. Since my preferences ran in a significantly different direction, and I had yet to learn how to recognize and avoid attention of this nature, I grew increasingly uncomfortable with Sheldon's generosity. As our day drew to a close, I was not sure what to expect. Did he want to kiss me? Did he expect something more? I must say that, while the day was enjoyable, I was relieved when I was dropped off at my hostel without confrontation.

I set out again later that evening, this time by myself, in search of dinner and some additional sightseeing. Although my agenda remained arbitrary, I managed to wind my way into districts that were popular with Parisians and tourists alike.

The Left Bank (Rive Gauche) was by far the most impressive, especially the narrow streets and obscured pathways that were punctuated by colorful little shops, festive lights and spirited cafes. In one section, a large number of restaurants were clustered tightly together, each presenting an impressive array of exquisitely prepared dishes with the hopes of capturing the attention of passers-by and luring them in for a meal. While these tempting presentations certainly attracted my attention, I lacked the experience to understand exactly how these restaurants operated. Finding myself in an entirely unfamiliar situation, amidst so many people speaking a language I could not understand, regardless how inviting these places seemed, I was clearly out of my depth.

Seeking a more familiar environment, I elected to patronize one of the many sidewalk vendors - in this case a small cart featuring both sweet (apple, berry, Nutella) and savory (ham, cheese, mushroom) crepes. While I was familiar with the concept, I had never tried anything like this before. With a preference for savory over sweet, I ordered a ham and gruyere crepe.

To my delight, it was hot, gooey, rich and cheesy, displaying a wonderfully soft texture that I simply adored. It was, second only to hot dogs, the best street food I had ever consumed. Feeling happy and nourished, I returned to the hostel to contemplate my options for the foreseeable future.

While I was willing to stumble around the city for several more days, I felt an obligation to give Frommer's a little credence and check out some of the iconic landmarks that had been highlighted within its pages - Notre-Dame, Eiffel Tower, Louvre, Champs-Élysées, Centre Pompidou, Arc de Triomphe, Latin Quarter, etc. Considering the abundance of baguette, crepe, pastry, confectionery, and coffee vendors along the way, I snacked frequently and was elated with every bite. Needless to say, I did not go hungry.

One of the most satisfying culinary moments took place when I discovered hot roasted chestnuts. Since I'd seen something similar in New York but never indulged, and as long as I was already taking so many chances and making each day an adventure, I elected to give these smoky little nuggets a try.

I must admit that trying to walk, pay appropriate attention to traffic, take in the sights, juggle the bag, and crack open chestnuts all at the same time was a true test of coordination. The reward, however, was ecstasy, making me a huge fan of chestnuts. Even today, I'll still buy chestnuts from street vendors whenever encountered and enjoy cooking with them at home.

Overall, Paris broadened my culinary vocabulary, bolstered my confidence, and helped me become a better informed traveler. Through the kindness of strangers, restaurateurs, retailers, and my guidebook, I managed to explore the French capital without major upset, enjoyed remarkable sensory experiences, and made indelible memories that remain some of my most cherished.

Although I've returned to Paris on several occasions over the last few decades, dined in better restaurants, sampled astonishing assortments of cheese, pâté, pastries, and confectionery from one end of the city to the other, and cracked open countless bottles of French wine, none of these encounters has been as extraordinary. I guess it's akin to losing one's virginity. You never forget your first.

# CHICKEN LIVER PÂTÉ
## Serves 8

---

*INGREDIENTS*
1/2 lb. chicken livers
1/4 cup onion, thinly sliced
2 cloves garlic, crushed
1 bay leaf
1/2 teaspoon thyme
1/2 teaspoon Kosher salt
1/2 cup water
1 1/4 sticks unsalted butter, at room temperature
4 teaspoons brandy
1/2 teaspoon black pepper
1 baguette, sliced and toasted

*DIRECTIONS*
Place the chicken livers, onion, garlic, bay leaf, thyme, salt and water in a small saucepan and bring to a gentle boil. Immediately reduce the heat to low, stirring occasionally, until the livers are just cooked, about 3 minutes. Cover, remove from the heat, and let stand for 5 minutes.

Discard the bay leaf. Drain the liver mixture, then transfer to a food processor. With the motor running, add the butter, a little at a time, until it is fully incorporated. Add the brandy and pepper and continue processing until the mixture is completely smooth. Adjust the seasoning, as needed.

Transfer the pâté into a ramekin, cover with plastic wrap, making sure the wrap is pressed onto the surface of the pâté. Refrigerate overnight.

Serve with toasted baguette slices.

# HAM & GRUYERE CREPES
Makes 6 - 8 crepes

---

*INGREDIENTS*
2 large eggs
3/4 cup milk
1/2 cup water
1 cup flour
3 tablespoons melted butter, plus more for coating the pan
1/4 lb. gruyere, grated
1/4 lb. ham, chopped into small dice

*DIRECTIONS*
To make the pancake batter, whisk together the eggs, milk, water, flour, and melted butter in a large bowl.

Place a large flat griddle or frying pan over high heat. Rub the pan with butter, making sure to coat the entire surface.

Reduce the heat to medium high, then ladle enough batter to make a thin 12″ pancake. Use a spatula to spread out the batter or simply tilt the pan in all directions.

As the pancake cooks, it will become dry enough to lift out. This is when you sprinkle a little cheese and ham on half of the pancake. After a minute, and once the cheese has started to melt, fold the pancake in half so that the ham and cheese are completely covered. Continue cooking for another minute or until the pancake begins to brown. Transfer the crepe to a platter, fold in thirds to create a triangle, and serve.

NOTE: When purchased from street vendors, the folded crepe is wrapped in paper and eaten with hands.

# STREET BAGUETTE
## Serves 4

---

*INGREDIENTS*

1 baguette

Spreads (pick one)
apricot preserves
fig preserves
mayonnaise
Dijon mustard (country style)

Cheeses (pick one)
brie, thinly sliced
camembert, thinly sliced
gruyere, thinly sliced

Meats (pick one)
turkey, thinly sliced
ham, thinly sliced
prosciutto, thinly sliced

Vegetables (as desired)
romaine lettuce
arugula leaves
spinach leaves
tomato, thinly sliced
red onion, thinly sliced

*DIRECTIONS*

On the streets of Paris, the ingredients found in a baguette sandwich are as varied as the multitudes of vendors. Accordingly, the directions for making a proper Street Baguette allows for numerous combinations of meat, cheese, vegetables and spreads.

To start, split open the baguette lengthwise. From this point forward, the combination of ingredients is up to you.

Start by placing a generous amount of the desired spread on both sides of the bread, followed by one meat, one cheese and as many vegetables as you prefer.

Carefully close and cut into four equal lengths. Serve with a nice bottle of wine, then sit back, relax and enjoy.

 **ITALY** I ordered the tortellini and a glass of wine. When a 1-litre carafe arrived, I was not sure if I had bought the whole thing or would be paying by the glass. Not wanting to waste money, I simply drank the whole thing.

I visited a few places after Paris that were along the path towards Italy without much in the way of significance in terms of memories or culinary experience. There's no doubt that opportunities existed. I simply did not have the awareness, inclination, or experience to fully appreciate where I was or take full advantage of the delights that may have been available.

Considering that I had not yet become much of a drinker, collegiate overindulgences notwithstanding, I also missed out on most of the colorful and social opportunities that a lively bar or taproom would have provided. Ultimately, my travel consisted primarily of arrival by train, a brief orientation at the travel desk, securing a hotel, hostel or guest house for a couple of nights, and a few quick visits to well known tourist destinations. Meals tended to be incidental, limited to whatever I could afford, without much concern for truly ethnic experiences.

Shunning advance planning, and unless chance social inter-actions along the way provided companionship, I would be back on the road in relatively short time.

The fact that I visited Italy at all was based solely on recom-mendations from backpackers that I had met on various trains and in hostels when I first started out. It was my understanding that I simply had to visit Italy, especially the Uffizi Gallery in Florence. Rome was also mentioned as a must visit destination, especially one particular restaurant (I do not recall its name) that served a dish called "tortellini" that was supposedly beyond belief.

Were it not for the unbridled enthusiasm that accompanied these recommendations, I doubt I would have taken the time to visit this country, seek out the restaurant, or try the dish.

Needless to say, I was still quite clueless about international travel and had not yet acclimated to foreign cultures. In addition, the practice of using my passport, exchanging traveler's checks, and navigating public transport in exotic new lands was still a bit shaky. Fortunately, there were always travel offices at the train stations to help me get oriented, find suitable accommodations, purchase a map, and formulate how I would spend my time in the city. At the very least, I had acquired enough sense to obtain currency in advance of my arriving in whatever destination was next on my agenda.

It's important to keep in mind that my priorities at this stage in life centered more upon sex, drugs and rock-and-roll and encounters with individuals who shared similar interests. While I had certainly learned to appreciate and enjoy good food, and intriguing culinary experiences were welcomed, there were more pressing interests on my agenda. That being said, on those occasions when extraordinary foods were encountered, my senses would swing into high alert.

With the help of my handy-dandy guidebook and the insights I could glean from its pages, I set out for Florence. Upon arrival, and after the usual dealings with the tourist office and money exchange, I found a little pensione that would be perfect as my home base, not far from the Piazzale Michelangelo.

Once settled, I needed a little time for orientation. Keep in mind that I was hardly the ideal tourist, had not yet formulated an agenda, and was in Florence (and Italy) only because it had been energetically proclaimed by every backpacker I encountered as an essential destination. So here I was.

Sadly, I barely remember the Uffizi Gallery, completely overlooked the Ponte Vecchio bridge and the Cathedral of Santa Maria del Fiore, have no recollection of the Arno River (although I had to cross it to get from the Piazzale Michelangelo to the Uffizi), and cannot recall any meaningful social encounters. I do, however, have a vivid and enduring recollection of the wonderful pizzas and gelati I enjoyed during my stay.

For those of you who adore pizza, imagine a counter top that runs the entire length of the pizzeria. Now, cover this counter, from the front window all the way to the back wall, with tray upon tray of pizzas ready to be baked and served. From your basic margherita, pepperoni, mushroom, or sausage configurations to more exotic variations that included ricotta, kalamata olives, eggplant, anchovies, and prosciutto, we're talking about endless varieties to choose from. Of course, there were several with ingredients I had never encountered and could not possibly identify. It was, without a doubt, a pizza lover's dream come true. If Disneyland could be pizza, this was it.

Since it was so long ago, I have no idea if my encounter was authentic or simply something artfully contrived to impress the tourists. Considering most of the shops I patronized were adjacent to Piazzale Michelangelo, coupled with my youth and inexperience, they could have easily been colorfully articulated tourist traps. Coupled with the fact that, before I visited Italy, my exposure to pizza had been limited to neighborhood take-out joints and those available from the supermarket's freezer, I was naive enough to be easily impressed. Regardless, I found the pizzas in Florence remarkably decadent.

While the pizza was impressive, the ice cream was absolutely divine - the best thing ever. Instead of the somewhat ordinary varieties that I knew from American supermarkets, including the enticing varieties that BaskinRobbins and Swensen's (the leading ice cream retailers of the day) had to offer, the ice cream I experienced in Florence - known as gelati - was super rich, super thick, super creamy, and oh-my-god super delicious. Plus, there were exotic flavors like mango, passion fruit, and ginduja that were altogether new and provocative sensations.

Of course, I started with my longstanding favorite - chocolate. Yes! Yes! Yes! Then, as I wandered the city and encountered other gelati shops, I indulged in other heavenly flavors. Yes! Yes! Yes!

With pizza and gelati firmly established as my newfound dietary staples, it was time to expand my horizons, head south to Rome, and find out about this stuff called tortellini. Since I did not fully understand what a city like Rome would have to offer, I decided it would be easier to keep my room in Florence and make a day trip. Considering how easy it was to gallivant around the continent using my Eurail pass, I could take an early morning train, see the Colosseum, check out the pasta that should not be missed, and be back in Florence in time for an evening stroll, another slice of pizza, and a dish of gelati.

It's important to realize that, at this time in my life, the only pasta I knew about was either spaghetti (dry from a box) or Chef Boy-ar-dee ravioli (in tomato sauce from a can). We didn't use the word "pasta" at home. It was either "spaghetti" or "ravioli." Even macaroni was alien to the Spear household. I wouldn't come to appreciate the allure of macaroni & cheese, especially the cheap and easy-to-prepare version that comes in a bright blue box, until I moved to Los Angeles and started cooking on a limited budget. I didn't learn how to make truly magnificent mac-n-cheese until I moved to Florida (there's a recipe for Killer Mac-n-Cheese in the Jacksonville chapter).

So, bright and early the next day, I headed out to the train station eager to begin my day-long adventure in Rome. The good news is that the train was on time, I boarded, and we were off. The not so good news was that, in the process of trying to interpret the signs (written in Italian), I boarded a northbound train and spent the morning going in the wrong direction (Rome is south of Florence). As soon as I got to the first stop about an hour and a half away, I disembarked, found a return train to Florence, and returned to my pensione. I would attempt another day-trip the next morning.

After a good night's sleep, taking greater care in the morning, I headed out to the train station once again, boarded the correct train (this time) and found myself in Rome just a few hours later. By the time I arrived, it was nearly lunchtime. With tortellini a pressing desire, I made a beeline for the much acclaimed restaurant.

It was quiet when I arrived. As with evening meals throughout Europe, I simply assumed that lunchtime started later in the day and I had arrived a bit too early. Not wanting to delay any further, I simply sat down, asked for the menu, ordered the now infamous tortellini, and asked for a glass of wine. When a 1-litre carafe arrived, I was not sure if I had bought the whole thing or would be paying for however many glasses I consumed. Being too inexperienced, not speaking the language, more than a bit intimidated, and not wanting to waste money, I simply decided to drink the whole thing.

As I worked my way through the wine, the tortellini arrived. Having never encountered anything like this before, these plump little knobs of meat-filled pasta were definitely an eye opener. Never being one to shy away from intriguing new foods, I took a bite.

I was in love.

It was easy to understand why my traveling companions were so adamant about this dish. Delicious? Absolutely!

Between the wonderfulness of the tortellini, along with the aura of well-being, relaxation and subtle warmth that the near empty carafe of wine provided, lunch was a tremendously successful endeavor. With just the Colosseum remaining on my agenda for the day, and a glimpse of my map confirming that I would pass it along the way back to the train station, I paid my bill, extended my thanks, and began a very pleasant, albeit slightly unsteady, walk through the streets of Rome.

All I can tell you about the remainder of the day is that I did see the Colosseum. I arrived, stopping for about 30 seconds to take in the view (it looked just like every photo I'd ever seen), and continued on my way. I subsequently made it to the train station, got back to my pensione, and fell asleep.

As a matter of clarification, were I to visit Italy today (or any of the overseas destinations featured in the first half of this book), I would be conducting considerable online research and preparing an itinerary prior to travel. These days, I rarely travel without a sizable "to-do" list of cultural attractions, colorful neighborhoods, and acclaimed restaurants that I want to be sure to visit while on location. I am considerably more appreciative, although I have been known to maintain the tradition of consuming larger than average volumes of wine and walking with a bit of a wobble.

It's also important to mention that tortellini remains one of my all-time favorite pasta dishes, although Pappardelle al Ragu (check out the recipe in the Serbia chapter) is up at the top of my list as well.

# CHICKEN MILANESE
## Serves 4

---

*INGREDIENTS*
2 boneless chicken breasts (each cut in half, flat-wise)
1/4 cup milk
2 eggs, beaten
1 1/2 cups flour, for dredging
1 cup breadcrumbs, plain
1/4 cup Parmesan cheese, grated
1 tablespoon parsley, finely chopped (extra for garnish)
1 tablespoon garlic, finely minced
1 teaspoon salt
1 teaspoon pepper
1/2 cup olive oil
1 lemon, cut into 8 wedges

*DIRECTIONS*
Cut each chicken breast in half, flat-wise, then pound into thin, even pieces.

Place the flour in a shallow bowl. In a separate shallow bowl, whisk together the eggs and milk.

Place the breadcrumbs, Parmesan, parsley, garlic, salt and pepper in a third shallow bowl and mix thoroughly.

Dredge each cutlet in flour, then the eggs, followed by the breadcrumbs. Place each piece on a clean dry plate.

Heat the oil in a large skillet over medium heat. Cook the cutlets until golden brown, about 2 minutes per side.

To serve, garnish with a sprinkle of chopped parsley and two lemon wedges.

# LINGUINI WITH LEMON BASIL PESTO
### Serves 8

*INGREDIENTS*
1 1/2 cups fresh basil, stems removed, plus more for garnish
1 cup Italian parsley
1/2 cup pine nuts
2 cloves garlic
2 lemons, zested
1 cup olive oil
1 cup Parmesan, grated, plus more for garnish
salt, to taste
1 teaspoon lemon juice
2 lbs. linguini

*DIRECTIONS*
Place the basil, parsley, pine nuts, garlic, and lemon zest in a blender. With the motor running, add the olive oil, a little at a time, until a loose paste is formed. Add the Parmesan and, if needed, a little more oil. Mix in salt and lemon juice to taste.

Cook the linguini according to instructions, drain and place in a large bowl. Add the pesto and toss.

To serve, garnish with grated Parmesan and finely sliced strips (chiffonade) of fresh basil.

# PIZZA CON TUTTO
Makes 1 large or 3 small pizzas

*INGREDIENTS*
For the Dough
1 1/4 cups lukewarm water
1 teaspoon active dry yeast
1 teaspoon sugar
3 cups flour
1 1/4 teaspoons salt
4 tablespoons olive oil
(coarse cornmeal, for baking)

Toppings
These are just a few of the toppings you might enjoy on your pizza. How much of each is up to you.

| | |
|---|---|
| extra virgin olive oil | pepperoni |
| tomato paste (or sauce) | Italian sausage |
| finely sliced garlic | Parmesan cheese |
| fresh basil | ricotta cheese |
| sun-dried tomatoes | mozzarella cheese, fresh |
| Kalamata olives | red pepper flakes |
| mushrooms | roasted red pepper |

*DIRECTIONS*
For the Dough
Using a small bowl, mix together the water, yeast, and sugar. Let sit for 5 minutes (you should see bubbles forming).

In a large bowl, combine the flour and salt, then drizzle in the oil and water to form a dough. Knead the dough for about 5 minutes, then cover and rest (the dough will rise slightly).

After 45 minutes, transfer the dough to the refrigerator, allowing it to rise even further overnight.

To Assemble
Preheat the oven to 450°F.

If you are making small pizzas, divide the dough into three equal portions and roll each into a ball. Using a well floured surface, roll the dough to the desired size and thickness.

Once the dough has been rolled, brush a little olive oil over the surface, followed by whatever toppings you prefer.

Sprinkle a little corn meal into a baking tray or pizza pan (this allows a little heat to get under the crust and crisp it up a bit. It also makes it easier to remove the pizza.). Using a pizza paddle (peel), transfer the pizza to the prepared pan, then bake for 10 to 15 minutes, allowing the crust to get golden brown and crispy and the toppings hot and bubbling.

Remove from the oven, cut into slices, and serve.

# TORTELLINI WITH SPICY MEAT SAUCE
## Serves 8

---

*INGREDIENTS*
1/4 cup olive oil
2 teaspoons garlic, minced
1/2 cup carrot, finely chopped
2 red capsicums, finely chopped
1 lb. Italian sausage (hot), casings removed
1 cup dry red wine
1 can (28oz) crushed tomatoes
1 cup water, more if needed
salt, pepper and sugar, to taste
1 teaspoon crushed red pepper (optional)
1 lb. cheese tortellini (fresh, not dried)
grated Parmesan, as desired
fresh basil chiffonade (for garnish)

*DIRECTIONS*
Pour the olive oil into the bottom of a large Dutch oven. Over medium high heat, sauté the garlic briefly, then add the carrot and capsicum. Cook until the vegetables are soft, about 10 minutes. Add the sausage and continue cooking until all excess liquid has evaporated. Using the back of a spoon, break up any large lumps of meat. Add the wine and continue cooking until dry once again.

Add the crushed tomatoes followed by the water, salt, pepper and sugar, to taste. If you like a spicy sauce, add the crushed red pepper. Bring to a boil, then reduce to simmer, cooking for about 30 minutes. Add more water (or wine), as needed, to maintain a saucy consistency.

While the sauce is cooking, prepare the tortellini according to the directions on the package.

Once the sauce is done and the pasta is fully cooked, divide the pasta equally between four bowls. Spoon a healthy amount of sauce over top, followed by a generous sprinkle of Parmesan. Garnish with basil and serve while still hot.

---

*"Fish, to taste right, must swim
three times - in water, in butter and in wine."*
*Polish Proverb*

---

**LONDON**

This was deep-fried pieces of steaming hot deliciousness served with a generous scoop of chips, all shoveled into a hand rolled cone of butcher's paper.

Compared to Paris and Italy, London was considerably easier for me to explore and enjoy. Quite simply, the street signs, tourist literature, menus, and everything else I encountered were in English. Of course, I was still a newbie in terms of travel-related skills. Finding a hotel, eating in restaurants, and generally comporting myself appropriately in public places was still a work in progress.

I did, however, manage to wander the banks of the River Thames, listen as Big Ben struck the hour, see incredible artworks at the Tate Gallery, marvel at the Crown Jewels in the Tower of London, and feed more pigeons than I had ever seen in one place in Trafalgar Square.

As with Italy, the memories that endure have nothing to do with these well-known tourist attractions - although I vividly recall buying a very nice gift for my parents from the Wedgwood store in Piccadilly circus - a black & white striped Jasperware urn. It was, at the time, the most expensive impulse purchase I had ever made and is a treasure among the Spear family jewels.

This being said, the bulk of the experiences from London that remain clear in my mind and continue to bring a smile to my face today are entirely culinary.

For those of you who grew up listening to Jethro Tull's "Aqualung" (released in 1971), there is a song called "Up to Me." At the start of the song, the lyrics include a line "...leave you in a Wimpy Bar..." that I never quite understood. Once I started wandering the streets of London and spotted a hamburger joint called Wimpy Bar, I immediately came to grips with the lyrics. What became crystal clear is that J. Wellington Wimpy, the portly man who appeared in Popeye cartoons dressed in a suit and bowler hat offering to "gladly pay you on Tuesday for a hamburger today" had a UK-based fast food franchise named in his honor. (Note: I have subsequently learned that the Wimpy brand originated in Chicago as a chain of hamburger restaurants called Wimpy Grills. It was subsequently licensed to an operator in the UK who changed the name to Wimpy Bar.)

Since my culinary preferences in Europe tended to favor foods and flavors that were new and intriguing, and being quite familiar with fast food hamburgers, I never patronized the Wimpy Bar. That being said, every time I saw one of these places, the song would immediately come to mind and a smile would cross my face. When you consider that "Aqualung" was one of the very first albums I ever owned, and played it incessantly, gaining insight to the lyrics was a very happy occasion.

While I did not arrive with any pre-conceived notions about

British food, or a list of must-try dishes indigenous to the UK, my adventures introduced me to several iconic dishes that remain some of my all-time favorites today.

It all started with a midday stroll. Noticing a line of people spilling out onto the sidewalk from a corner shop just up the road, and a parade of happy patrons passing by with some kind of a meal served in a large, rolled up paper cone, I was intrigued. Other than the impressive stream of patrons coming and going, this shop was inconspicuous, well-worn, and turned out to be nothing more than a simply organized fast food joint specializing in fish and chips.

Established as a take-away business, there were no tables - just a menu board on the wall, a high topped service counter, and an enormous bath tub-like contraption lining the back wall that was the largest deep fryer I had ever seen. Nearly as wide as the store itself, there was enough room in this cauldron of hot oil to cook dozens of meals at a single time with plenty of wiggle room for busy staff to maneuver.

While not particularly hungry, I am one of those people who, when presented with an opportunity to try enticing new foods, can always eat. So, I joined the queue and launched myself into a new culinary adventure (Yes, I was starting to become culturally aligned). They wait in queues in Britain, not lines. They also enjoy chips, not French fries; biscuits, not cookies; scones, not biscuits; there are pips in their orange juice, not seeds; and they drive on the wrong side of the road - a fact I learned quite quickly after looking the wrong way, stepping out onto the street, and nearly being flattened by a very large British taxi).

Other than new surroundings, I quickly realized this fish bore no resemblance to the pre-fab, precisely formed, breaded, and quick frozen fish favored by American fast food operators. This was strips of fresh fish, batter-dipped, and deep-fried to order, forming golden, crispy, crunchy, and irregularly formed pieces of steaming hot deliciousness served with a generous scoop of chips, all shoveled into a hand rolled cone of butcher's paper filled to overflowing.

Don't ask me how many different varieties of fish and seafood were on the menu or how much I paid. I simply don't remember. What I do recall is gleefully walking out of the place with this monumental serving of fish and chips. Too hot too eat, I walked down the street in search of a place to sit. Without going very far, I found a well-maintained park with some benches, made myself at home, and chowed down. No intimidating wait staff. No cutlery. No formality. Just me, the green grass, sunny blue skies, and my treasure trove of fish, fat, salt, and flavor.

This encounter with fried seafood would not be the only noteworthy culinary experience in London. Although my guidebook was steering me towards cultural institutions, landmarks of distinction, and postcard perfect surroundings, I found myself attracted more to repositories of all things edible. This was certainly the case when I visited Harrod's and discovered they operated one of the most fanciful, exquisite, and enticing food halls I had ever seen.

First, it's important to understand that this was nothing like the fast food courts that have become mainstay operations in American shopping malls. This was a gourmet food shoppers paradise endowed with endless aisles of esoteric and exotic delicacies imported from all over the world. There was also a long line of glass-fronted service counters displaying an array of wild game and dry-cured meats, sweet baked goods of every possible design, and fanciful confections unlike any I'd seen before.

It wasn't just the affluence of exotic foods that was so impressive. It was the way in which elegance, sophistication, and creativity were consistently employed throughout the store.

Most notable were the displays of wild game that adorned the main entrance. There were wildly plumed birds, large and small, ornately posed as if in flight, casually encircling platters of suckling pig, carved meats, and other such fanciful foods, all presented on multi-tiered displays nestled amidst a profusion of vibrantly hued floral arrangements. The net effect was a tableau reminiscent of the most detailed Renaissance-era still life paintings.

Needless to say, the temptation to try just about everything in sight was considerable. Remembering that I was traveling on a tight budget, and many of these delicacies were well beyond my capacity to afford, I opted for just two uniquely British foods - a Cornish pasty and a Scotch egg. since I had never encountered either of these foods before, the server behind the counter had to explain them.

Similar to an empanada, I learned that the Cornish pasty is a shortcrust pastry filled with meat, vegetables, and a few spices. As it was explained, this hearty handheld "pie" was originally prepared as a convenient lunch for workers in the mining community of Cornwall. Considering the only handheld pie I had ever consumed was a sickly sweet fried apple concoction from McDonald's, the idea of a beef and potato filling inside a baked pie crust sounded far better.

The other item I purchased was a Scotch egg. While there are many theories about how the Scotch egg came to be, and no one story seems to hold sway, its origins are undoubtedly British. Described as a hard boiled egg, wrapped in sausage, coated in bread crumbs, and subsequently deep fried, this was too unusual to ignore. Yes please!

With my culinary treasures in hand, having exceeded my quota for food purchases for the day, I found my way back onto the streets of London for a wander and a nosh. Let's just say that I wasted no time, greedily devouring both the pasty and the egg without hesitation.

Should you find yourself feeling a wee bit peckish, whether in Britain or a home-town British pub, I highly recommend both of these wonderfully satisfying snacks.

Of course, there were the obligatory bangers with mash and peas. It's important for me to qualify my preference as follows: Any food prepared in a sausage format, from hot dogs and Slim Jim's to soppressata and finocchiona, are always happily consumed. Going one step further, just about anything served with a healthy portion of mashed potatoes is always welcomed on my plate. So, go ahead and add Shepherd's Pie to my list of worthwhile British dishes as well.

If you had any doubts, I also strayed into a pub or two along the way. After all, I had frequented bars, discos and clubs at home but had never set foot in a British pub. Considering there were always wonderfully brewed local beers to sample, curious signage adorning the walls, interesting programs on the "telly," and intriguing accents and conversations to overhear, taking in the sights and sounds of London through the bottom of a glass was tremendously rewarding.

My preferred cocktails at the time were either 7&7 (Seagram's 7 and 7-Up) or rum & Coke. In some of the pubs I would visit, instead of beer, I would slosh down a few of these. To my dismay, ice was not something the Brits favored (a habit left over from WWII when ice was scarce). Whenever I ordered a drink, and only if I asked, I would get a cube or two but that's all. Compared to the drinks I was used to at home, all heaped full of ice, this was something I found difficult to accept. Considering the disapproving looks I got when asking for more ice, I adapted quickly.

I visited a few more countries while exploring Europe on $10 a day. When you consider that I made no advance plans, and I was not terribly inquisitive about local delicacies (that would happen later in life), the next chapter of groundbreaking culinary enlightenment would not take place until I returned home and settled into my very first apartment at the beach in The City of Angels - Los Angeles, California.

# BRITISH BANGERS
Makes 8 skinless sausages

---

*INGREDIENTS*
1 egg, beaten
1/2 cup breadcrumbs, toasted
1/2 teaspoon black pepper
1/2 teaspoon kosher salt
1/2 teaspoon rubbed sage
1/4 teaspoon nutmeg
1/4 teaspoon cayenne pepper
2 tablespoons fresh parsley, finely chopped
1/4 cup water
1 pound lean ground beef (or 1/2 lb. beef, 1/2 lb. pork)
2 tablespoons peanut oil

*DIRECTIONS*
Whisk the eggs thoroughly, then mix in the breadcrumbs, pepper, salt, sage, nutmeg, cayenne and parsley.

Using your hands to add the meat, take care to fully incorporate the ingredients. Cover and refrigerate for 2 hours.

After 2 hours, mix once again to ensure a consistent blend, then divide the mixture into 8 equal portions. Roll each portion into a 6-inch long sausage shape.

To cook, pour the oil into a frying pan over medium high heat. Fry the sausages, turning every couple of minutes, until nicely browned on all sides.

Serve over mashed potatoes with a side of buttered peas (Bangers & Mash) or in a bread roll smothered with sautéed onions and a smear of Dijon mustard.

# OVEN-FRIED CHIPS
Serves 6

---

*INGREDIENTS*
2 lb. potatoes
3 tablespoons olive oil
1 teaspoon Kosher salt
1 teaspoon black pepper
1 teaspoon fresh thyme leaves, finely chopped

*DIRECTIONS*
Preheat oven to 400°F.

Wash and dry the potatoes. Cut each potato lengthwise into 1/2-inch slices, then cut each slice into 1/2-inch chips.

In a large bowl, toss the potatoes with the olive oil, followed by the salt, pepper and thyme. Transfer to a large baking tray and bake for 20 minutes. Turn the potatoes and bake for another 20 minutes until they are nicely browned and crispy.

Serve immediately.

# PANKO CRUSTED FISH
## Serves 4

---

*INGREDIENTS*
<u>Lemony Fish Sauce</u>
1/2 cup mayonnaise
zest of 1 lemon
juice of 1 lemon
1/2 teaspoon dill

<u>Coatings</u>
1 cup flour
1 1/2 teaspoons kosher salt
1 1/2 teaspoons garlic powder
1 teaspoon cayenne
1 teaspoon black pepper
1 egg
1/4 cup water
2 cups panko
4 cod filets (approximately 1/2 lb. each), towel dried, then cut in half lengthwise
vegetable oil for frying

<u>To Serve</u>
2 cups shredded lettuce
1 teaspoon dill, for garnish

*DIRECTIONS*
Make the Lemony Fish Sauce: mix all of the ingredients together in a small bowl, then cover and refrigerate.

Prepare the coatings using three large, shallow mixing bowls. In the first, whisk together the flour, salt, garlic powder, black pepper, and cayenne. In the second, whisk the egg and water until fully mixed. Place the panko in the third.

Dredge the fish fillets, one at a time, in the flour mixture, followed by the egg wash, and finally the panko, making sure the fillet is thoroughly coated. Place the coated fillets on a large plate and set aside.

To cook, drizzle a little oil in the bottom of a large frying pan. Cook each fillet over medium high heat for about 7-8 minutes until nicely browned. Turn the fish over and cook for an additional 7-8 minutes. Add more vegetable oil, as needed.

To serve, place the fish on top of a bed of shredded lettuce drizzled with a small amount of Lemony Fish Sauce. Garnish with a sprinkle of dill.

NOTE: This fish pairs perfectly with Oven Fried Chips.

---

*"If you're afraid of butter, use cream."*
*Julia Child*

---

# SCOTCH EGGS
### Makes 4 eggs

---

*INGREDIENTS*
2 quarts vegetable oil, for frying
6 eggs, divided
2 teaspoons kosher salt
1 teaspoon crushed red pepper
1 teaspoon sugar
1 teaspoon black pepper, freshly ground
1 teaspoon sage
1 teaspoon thyme
1/2 teaspoon cayenne
1/4 cup water
1 1/2 lb. ground pork
3/4 cup flour
3/4 cup panko*
English mustard, for serving

*DIRECTIONS*
Place 4 eggs in a saucepan and cover with water. Bring to a boil, then continue cooking for 12 minutes. Transfer the eggs to a bowl of ice water. Once cooled, peel and set aside.

To make the sausage, mix together the salt, red pepper, sugar, black pepper, sage, thyme, and cayenne. Add the water and mix, then add the pork. Knead this mixture together until the water and spices are thoroughly incorporated. Cover and chill for one hour.

Pour the oil into the deep fryer and pre-heat to 375°F.

Roll the sausage into a log and divide into 4 equal pieces. Using one portion of sausage, flatten it to form a thin patty.

Place the egg at one end of the patty, then roll the sausage up and over the egg so that it covers it entirely. Press the meat firmly around the egg, making sure it is entirely encased. Repeat this process with each egg.

Set up three shallow bowls. Place flour in one, the panko in another, and the two remaining eggs, beaten, in the third.

Roll the wrapped eggs, one at a time, in the flour, making sure to coat the entire surface, then in the egg, followed by the panko. Make sure you have an even coating of panko over the entire surface.

Deep-fry the eggs in batches, taking care not to crowd them, for 5 minutes. Once the eggs are fully cooked and golden brown, transfer to a dish lined with paper towels and allow to drain.

Serve warm with a generous dollop of English mustard.

*Panko is Japanese style breadcrumbs, available at most supermarkets and Asian grocery stores.

 An order of chili fries topped with cheese and lots of grated onions was always satisfying, especially in the wee hours when a greasy remedy for a few too many cocktails was desperately needed.

**A**fter three months of European adventures, the time had come to return to America, confirm a career agenda, and decide where I wanted to live. With a Bachelor of Fine Arts degree and a specialty in graphic design under my belt, a career in design was obvious. With the desire to achieve great things, I knew it would be important to relocate to either Chicago, New York, or Los Angeles, considered the top markets for designers at the time. After four years in Tucson and the Arizona desert, I had become quite acclimated to, and developed a preference for, warmer weather. Considering that Chicago and New York both had what I considered horrible winters, a move to Los Angeles was the only logical choice.

Living on my own in a city the size of LA, without a roommate or parental supervision, was challenging at the start. With only $300 to my name, and low wages paid to entry level designers, I started out in a small, one-room, rent-controlled apartment in Santa Monica just a few blocks from the beach.

Without money for furniture, shelving was created from milk crates, upended cinder blocks stood in for chairs, and a borrowed chaise lounge mattress would stand in as my bed until I could afford something better. Fortunately, I had a small folding table which served as my desk and dining room table.

Lacking practiced skills in the kitchen, I started out simply with a can opener, bottle opener, soup pot, frying pan and a few utensils. The meals I managed to pull together consisted of easy-to-make dishes such as fried eggs, canned corned beef hash, spaghetti with store bought sauce, tuna salad, peanut butter & jelly sandwiches, and boxed macaroni & cheese. Needless to say, a significant number of hot meals also came from inexpensive fast-casual operations in the neighborhood.

Discovering that boxed mac-n-cheese could be made considerably better with a little bit of real cheddar grated in, this configuration became a mainstay. I also found it could be enhanced with ingredients such as sautéed green peppers and ground beef. Recognizing these additions could not truly improve upon this food, my friends and I started referring to any dish that started with a blue box as "macaroni slime."

When it came to dining out during my first few years in LA, the most noteworthy dishes were street food. Along with burritos, tacos, subs, and pizza were chili dogs, chili burgers, and chili fries.

If you have not had the pleasure, nothing beats a chili dog (served with mustard, chili, and finely chopped onions) from Pink's, an iconic hot dog emporium on North La Brea Ave near Hollywood. Open all day, Pink's would provide welcomed sustenance for lunch as well as late night snacks.

It was my understanding that the best chili burger (a double cheeseburger with tomato, pickles, onion, ketchup, mustard, and chili) would be found at Tommy's on the corner of Beverly Blvd and Rampart, just a stone's throw from Dodger stadium. To say these burgers were a bit messy and should be eaten carefully is an understatement. That being said, they were ample reward for the considerable trek from Santa Monica.

When it came to chili fries, having sampled more than my fair share from vendors all over town, it became evident that the chili was never going to be an authentic chili con carne but more of a chili glop - something thick and red with meaty bits that bore a passing resemblance to the real deal. This being said, an order of chili fries topped with cheese and lots of grated onions was always satisfying, especially in the wee hours when a greasy remedy for a few too many cocktails was desperately needed.

It's important to note that, whether you choose chili dogs, chili burgers or chili fries, do not allow them to get cold and never, ever, take them home to consume later. While I will eat just about any leftover substance lingering in the fridge from the night before, there is nothing nastier than fast food chili glop left alone and given time to coagulate. Just say no!

There are, of course, other fast casual places to get good hamburgers around town. While many locals are outspoken devotees of In-N-Out Burger, I remain a staunch advocate of The Apple Pan on Pico Boulevard in West Los Angeles. Whether you order their Steakburger or Hickoryburger (served with a house made sauce, mayonnaise, pickles, and lettuce), they are meaty servings of wonderfulness. Along with Pink's and Tommy's, The Apple Pan is one of my all time favorite destinations for "good grease," the term I coined to describe these sorts of casual, yet satisfying, comfort foods.

While no longer in operation, Hamptons (on Highland Avenue in Hollywood) was a bit more upscale. Named after the vacation destination on Long Island, Hamptons was popular for lunch among the entertainment crowd working at nearby television and film studios. For me, it was simply a great place to get a really good burger. With an extensive menu ranging from the familiar to the exotic, my favorite was the Peppercorn Burger (topped with sautéed onions and peppercorns).

Los Angeles is also the place where I discovered dim sum. With its sizable Asian population, and a dynamic Chinatown adjacent to the city center, there were several highly recommended Chinese restaurants to choose from. Although it would take a few years to try them all, every outing was an eagerly awaited occasion. Time and time again, I would marvel at the enormity of the dining rooms, the numbers of people jostling for seats, the seemingly endless parade of push carts piled high with bamboo and stainless steel steamers, and the altogether unfamiliar yet intriguing configurations of food.

While I came to prefer siu mai (pork dumplings), har gow (shrimp dumplings), and wu gok (fried taro dumplings), the heady mix of sights, sounds, textures, aromas, and flavors was always exhilarating. Simply stated, going out for dim sum was probably the most fun I had ever had with food and launched a life-long obsession with Asian dumplings.

While I can no longer remember the names of the restaurants I frequented, there were a few other foods that made indelible impressions. These are the dishes that I ordered regularly and, over time, would learn how to make at home.

The simplest of these was a cream cheese & olive omelet that was served at one of my favorite brunch destinations in Venice Beach. Having grown up on cream cheese & olive sandwiches, the ingredients were familiar. What impressed me the most was the way in which the eggs and softened cream cheese interacted when subjected to heat. Plus, this place used a lot of cream cheese in the dish. Considering I can eat the stuff straight from the package without hesitation, the omelet was perfectly prepared.

Another standout was the potato salad served at one of my favorite sandwich places on Wilshire Boulevard on the outskirts of downtown. As with Tommy's, the distance was too great to visit on a regular basis. That being said, whenever I could manage, their oversized grilled cheese sandwiches and spicy potato salad were always worth the drive.

It's important to explain that I tend to crave anything made with mayonnaise - potato salad being my favorite. My mom made a basic potato salad with mayo, yellow mustard, celery, salt and pepper. The potato salad at this place had two advantages. The first was bigger chunks of potatoes that gave it substance. The second was a surprising touch of spice driven heat.

After several visits, and not being able to identify the special ingredient that gave this dish its heat, I finally asked the owner what he did to make his potato salad so good. While the recipe was not much different to my Mom's, the heat was attributed to dry powdered mustard in place of the prepared yellow stuff. I have since reformulated my own recipe and have been making potato salad with dry mustard ever since.

There was one other dish that I would be introduced to that would become one of my lifelong favorites - cold sesame noodles. When I saw this dish on the menu, knowing how much I enjoyed leftover spaghetti straight from the fridge for breakfast, I figured it warranted further investigation. While not terribly familiar with the Asian ingredients, the blend of sesame, ginger, onion, and garlic proved to be a winning combination. It would probably take another twenty years before I learned to make this dish for myself. That being said, I have come to love cold noodles in many configurations. And yes, cold leftover spaghetti in the morning, even before my first cup of coffee, remains a favorite today.

I have to give credit to my friends Ernie and Pam for much of the culinary awakening that I experienced in the City of Angels. I met Ernie on a racquetball court. Once we had bonded as friends, and realized we both enjoyed good food, we shared remarkable home-cooked meals (prepared by Pam) as well as countless culinary adventures all over town.

From an outside perspective, you would think the three of us never stopped eating or drinking. Every time we heard about great food being served, or a hot new restaurant opening its doors, the three of us were there. At the same time, I had also become a bit more adventurous in my own kitchen, acquiring significantly better cooking tools, and learning how to make more than just mac-n-cheese (although an abundance of those blue boxes would still inhabit my pantry). Of course, Ernie and Pam were always willing to try my latest culinary creations. While I would win their praise on many occasions, my cooking was never as good as anything Pam could make.

When it came to home cooking, my culinary breakthrough

can be directly attributed to The Silver Palate Cookbook by Julee Rosso & Sheila Lukins. What impressed me the most was the ease in which I could follow the recipes as well as all the notes in the margins that provided valuable insights and tips. Needless to say, I relied heavily on this book for just about every dinner party I hosted for many years.

The first dish I made using this book was Pasta with Sausage and Peppers. For accomplished cooks, the recipe is relatively simple, relying on commonplace ingredients that are staples in well-stocked kitchens. For me, everything about its preparation was an eye-opening education. The results, confirmed by the handful of friends who were willing to risk their lives on my first foray into "gourmet cuisine," were spectacular. When you consider that, prior to cooking from this book, my only skills were frying eggs, boiling water, and opening jars, producing this level of deliciousness was nothing short of miraculous.

The best dish I would ever learn to make was Chili Con Carne, based on a version made by my good friend and neighbor Ivy. Hers was a truly remarkable, richly satisfying, flavorful, and hearty dish that she pulled together without a recipe. Over time, making myself available to watch and write down what she used on numerous occasions, I was able to formulate my own recipe.

After a while, my chili would become the one dish I made that was a real crowd pleaser, so much so that I decided to enter it in the star-studded Malibu Chili Cook-off. Sponsored by the Malibu Kiwanis, hosted by Larry Hagman (I Dream of Jeannie, Dallas) and Julie Christie (Heaven Can Wait, Shampoo), and judged by a panel of Hollywood celebrities including Glen Frey, Mick Fleetwood and Cheech Marin, the cook-off was a lively and well attended affair officially sanctioned by the International Chili Society (ICS).

According to the rules, each chili chef could have two assistants (I nominated Ernie & Pam) and everything had to be prepared on-site. As such, and to liven things up, I named my chili "Spear's Original Southern California Style E-Ticket Chili (Disneyland used to have tickets for all of its rides - the really big roller-coasters required an "E" ticket), printed up t-shirts, invited lots of friends, and brought a half-gallon bottle of tequila. After each stage of cooking, we would celebrate with a shot of tequila. All of the meat and vegetables chopped... shot of tequila. Everything in the pot and simmering... shot of tequila. The chili is ready for final seasoning... shot of tequila. Chili finished and handed off to the judges... shot of tequila. Having a good time... you get the idea.

Along with the enthusiastic crowds, elephant rides, lively music, and dancing, it was a wonderful day. Yes, I met Larry and Julie and I cooked for some of the biggest names in Hollywood. That being said, although my chili did not win (I think it was the tequila), the cook-off remains one of my fondest memories from LA.

Over time, I learned how to make a few other dishes but never truly embraced the idea of cooking or entertaining at home. While LA would provide opportunities for my culinary vocabulary to grow, this resulted more from the many great restaurants I patronized as well as the specialty and ethnic food stores around town that offered prepared foods.

# CHILI CON CARNE
## Serves 10

---

*INGREDIENTS*
4 tablespoons olive oil
2 cups onion, finely chopped
4 jalapeno peppers, seeded, finely chopped
4 Anaheim peppers, seeded, finely chopped
2 serrano chilies, seeded, finely chopped
1 habanero chili, seeded, finely chopped
2 tablespoons garlic, minced
2 lb. brisket, cut into 1-inch cubes
2 lb. pork loin, cut into 1-inch cubes
3 cups water
2 tablespoons beef bouillon
4 bay leaves
3 tablespoons cumin, ground
1 tablespoon cumin seed
2 teaspoons mustard powder
1 teaspoon crushed red pepper
1/2 teaspoon cayenne
3 teaspoons salt
28 oz. crushed tomatoes (1 can)
3 tablespoons Worcestershire sauce
1 tablespoon unsweetened chocolate powder
12 oz. tomato paste
1 1/2 lb. dark red kidney beans (optional)
Tabasco, to taste

*DIRECTIONS*
Pour the olive oil in the bottom of a very large soup pot over
medium high heat. Add the onions, jalapeno, Anaheim,

serrano and habanero chilis and garlic and saute for 5 minutes until soft. Add the brisket and pork, making sure to brown the meat on all sides.

Add the water, bouillon and bay leaves and bring to a boil. Immediately reduce the heat to a simmer. Stir in the cumin, cumin seed, mustard, red pepper, cayenne and salt. Cook for 1 1/2 hours, stirring occasionally, adding more water as needed.

After 1 1/2 hours, add the crushed tomatoes, Worcestershire sauce and chocolate. Continue cooking for 1 to 1 1/2 hours, until the meat starts falling apart into shreds.

Stir in the tomato paste (and beans, if desired) and cook for another 15 minutes.

Add Tabasco and salt, to taste.

Serve with grated cheddar, sour cream, and saltine crackers.

# COLD SESAME NOODLES
## Serves 2 - 4

---

*INGREDIENTS*
1/2 lb. thin spaghetti
1/4 cup rice vinegar
1/4 cup sesame tahini
2 tablespoons soy sauce
2 tablespoons honey
1 tablespoon toasted sesame oil
1 teaspoon chili-garlic sauce
1 teaspoon brown sugar
1 chicken breast, cooked and shredded
1/2 cup cucumber, seeded and cut into matchsticks
1/4 cup scallions, thinly sliced
1/4 cup cilantro leaves, coarsely chopped, for garnish

*DIRECTIONS*
Bring a large pot of water to a boil over high heat and cook the noodles until just tender. Using a colander, drain and rinse the noodles under cold water.

In a large bowl whisk together the vinegar, tahini, soy sauce, honey, sesame oil, chili-garlic sauce and brown sugar. Add the noodles and toss, making sure the sauce is evenly distributed. Place in the refrigerator and chill.

To serve, place an equal amount of noodles in each of four bowls, then top with shredded chicken, cucumber, scallions, and cilantro.

# CREAM CHEESE & OLIVE OMELET
### Makes 1 omelet

---

*INGREDIENTS*
2 oz. cream cheese, softened
1 tablespoon sour cream
2 tablespoons olives*, sliced; plus a little more for garnish
1 tablespoon butter
3 eggs, beaten
salt and pepper, to taste

*DIRECTIONS*
Place the cream cheese and sour cream in a small bowl, whisk together, fold in the olives, then set aside.

Melt the butter in a 12-inch frying pan over medium-high heat. Pour in the eggs, tilting the pan around so that the eggs coat the entire surface of the pan. As soon as the eggs begin to set, carefully spread the cream cheese mixture over one half of the omelet. Allow to cook 1 minute longer, then fold the eggs over to create a half circle omelet. Continue cooking for just a few moments so the filling is warmed, then remove from the pan.

Garnish with a few more slices of olive and serve while hot.

* Make a Lox and Cream Cheese Omelet by substituting the olives with 2 tablespoons of chopped smoked salmon.

# WHITE POTATO SALAD
## Serves 8

*INGREDIENTS*

2 lb. red potatoes

1 cup mayonnaise

4 teaspoons cider vinegar

1 tablespoon grated onion

2 teaspoons black pepper

2 teaspoons celery salt

*DIRECTIONS*

Peel and cut the potatoes into 1/2 inch cubes.

Bring a large pot of water to a boil. Carefully add the potatoes, avoiding splashes of hot water, and cook for 10-15 minutes, until just tender. Drain, rinse with cold water to stop cooking and drain again.

In a large bowl, whisk together the mayonnaise, vinegar, onion, pepper, celery salt and salt. Fold in the drained potatoes, making sure they are fully incorporated, then cover and chill for 1 hour.

After 1 hour, stir the potato salad and test for flavor. Season to taste, then refrigerate overnight.

Note: This recipe is best when chilled overnight, allowing all of the flavors to fully mix, mingle and blend.

# PEPPERCORN CRUSTED BURGERS
## Makes 4

---

*INGREDIENTS*
2 tablespoons olive oil
4 cups Vidalia onion (sweet), thinly sliced
1 lb. ground beef
4 tablespoons black peppercorns, coarsely ground
4 hamburger rolls
4 oz. arugula

*DIRECTIONS*
Prepare a charcoal grill, bringing the heat up to a proper cooking temperature.

Pour the oil in the bottom of a large non-stick frying pan. Over medium heat, toss in the onions. Cook the onions slowly, tossing frequently to avoid burning, until nicely caramelized and brown. When fully cooked, remove from the heat and set aside.

Divide the beef into 4 equal portions, then form each into a patty approximately 1/2" thick.

Spread the peppercorns out on the bottom of a plate or shallow dish. Press the patties into the pepper, making sure to coat the flat surfaces as well as the sides.

When the grill is hot, cook the burger patties on one side for about 6 minutes, then flip and cook for 6 minutes longer.

Place one burger on each of the hamburger rolls, then top with a generous spoonful of caramelized onion followed by a quarter portion of the arugula. Serve immediately with ketchup, mustard, and/or mayonnaise.

# RIGATONI WITH SPICY SAUSAGE
## Serves 8

---

*INGREDIENTS*
1 tablespoon olive oil
1 1/2 cups onion, chopped
2 teaspoons garlic, minced
2 lb. spicy Italian sausage, casings removed
1/2 cup red wine
2 cans (28oz) crushed tomatoes
2 cups arugula, stems removed
1/2 cup fresh basil, chopped
1 tablespoon fresh oregano, chopped
salt, to taste
1 lb. rigatoni (dry)
Parmesan, grated, for serving

*DIRECTIONS*
For the sauce, pour the olive oil into the bottom of a large pot over medium high heat. Add the onions and garlic and sauté for 5 minutes. Add the sausage and cook for another 5 minutes, breaking up any large clumps. Add the wine and tomatoes, bring to a boil, then reduce to simmer and cover, cooking over low heat for 2 hours. Stir occasionally to avoid sticking or burning. Add wine or water, as needed.

Just before serving, stir in the arugula, basil and oregano and cook for 10 minutes. Add salt to taste, as needed.

Cook the rigatoni according to directions on the package. When done, drain and toss with a little olive oil.

To serve, place some rigatoni in a bowl, top with the sauce and sprinkle generously with Parmesan.

# SPICY POTATO SALAD
## Serves 12

---

*INGREDIENTS*
4 lb. red potatoes, peeled, cut into large dice
1 cup mayonnaise
2 teaspoons cider vinegar
3 teaspoons dry mustard powder
1/2 teaspoon salt
1/2 teaspoon black pepper
1/2 cup celery, finely chopped (optional)

*DIRECTIONS*
Place the diced potatoes in a large soup pot, adding enough cold water to cover by at least 1 inch. Bring to a boil, then simmer for approximately 15 minutes or until potatoes are just tender.

Drain the potatoes in a colander, rinsing several times with cold water to stop cooking. When fully drained, transfer to a large bowl and set aside.

In a small bowl, whisk together the mayonnaise, vinegar, mustard powder, salt and vinegar. Gently fold this mixture in with the potatoes until thoroughly incorporated. Cover and refrigerate.

After 3 hours, toss the potatoes and check for flavor, adding salt, pepper or any additional seasoning that may be desired. Return the salad to the refrigerator and chill for an additional 3 hours or overnight.

Toss the salad once again before serving.

The menu featured noodles, identified only by their Chinese names. Wanting to try them all, I simply started from the top and worked my way down.

**W**hile living in Los Angeles, I became enamored with the idea of living on a tropical island. With an opportunity to work in Hawaii, I packed up my meager belongings and moved to Oahu. Much to my dismay, I found that misleading promises had been made and the sun-kissed island life that I had expected was not going to work out. In just a few short weeks, realizing that so many things were not proceeding according to plan, I had to admit defeat and return to Los Angeles.

The good news is that, during this brief tenure, I cycled around Diamond Head, snorkeled in Hanauma Bay, and enjoyed the sun, sand and sights that Waikiki Beach and other parts of the coastline had to offer. I also found a handful of culinary delights that would influence my preferences for the rest of my life.

It's important to understand that groceries in Hawaii were very expensive (foods were not produced locally - everything in the supermarket was shipped in from the mainland) and my earning power was limited. As a result, the convenience and afford-ability of boxed macaroni and cheese ensured its prominence in the pantry and my daily diet.

With a craving for a fresh green salad every now and then, buying all of the ingredients at the supermarket turned out to be financially prohibitive. To my delight, a more affordable option was the all-you-can-eat salad bar at Sizzler Steakhouse. At a moment's notice, I could load up on leafy greens, assorted veggies, cottage cheese and fruit and go back for seconds (and even thirds) and walk away without breaking the bank.

Needless to say, mealtime at home was a sad affair. Based on the availability of prepared foods close to my Fort Street Mall office, the majority of my truly nutritional meals would be obtained during lunchtime.

Prior to my arrival on the Islands, my exposure to ethnic foods was limited. Recognizing a wide variety of Asian influences throughout Hawaii, mealtime quickly became an exciting and deliciously satisfying learning experience. Once introduced to bento (Japanese-style take-out), I would order either pork or chicken katsu, served up fresh, from a Japanese-owned food truck. While these dishes were good, I would spend consid-erably more time at the authentic Chinese restaurants within walking distance of my office.

Out of all these places, I spent most of my lunch hours in a little Chinese bakery conveniently situated on Hotel Street on the fringe of Chinatown. This tiny sliver of a restaurant sold take out dumplings and a curious variety of small baked goods from a service counter at the front of the store. Additionally, there were a handful of tables further inside where patrons could sit, order from a handwritten chalkboard menu, and enjoy their meal in-house.

The menu featured noodles, each dish paired with a specific combination of meats, vegetables and sauces. Identified only by their Chinese names, I had no idea what any of them might be. With a little help from the waiter, and wanting to try them all, I simply started from the top of the list and worked my way down, ordering a different dish each visit.

During my few weeks in residence, I sampled pan fried noodle dishes including gau gee mein (chicken and vegetables with thin egg noodles), niu chow fun (beef with wide rice noodles), and ha moon chow mai fun (shrimp and vegetables with thin rice noodles).

While I was completely unfamiliar with this style of Chinese cuisine and ordered blindly, noodles have always been, and continue to be, one of my favorite food groups. As such, working my way through the bakery's menu was an eagerly anticipated and deliciously exotic adventure.

Of course, ever since I was introduced to dim sum in Los Angeles, I never pass up an opportunity to enjoy Chinese dumplings. Since they were prominently featured on the bakery shelves in the shop's front window, I regularly ordered a plate of three or four steamed siu mai to go with whatever noodle dish I selected.

There were several other Chinese restaurants, primarily noodle houses, that served up similar dishes as well as ramen (noodle soup), wor wonton soup (noodles and wontons in broth), and cha chiang mein (noodles in brown meat sauce). While the ramen and wonton soups were good, and worthwhile variations could be found around town, there was only one restaurant that served cha chiang mein. Also called cha cha mein and zha jiang mian, this dish is best described as Asian Bolognese. While I have found other noodle dishes that are similar (dan dan mein being the most common), I have yet to find a noodle dish equal to the one I enjoyed in Honolulu.

I've also tried making cha chiang mein at home based on a handful of recipes I've found in books and online. Sadly, none have lived up to my expectations. While the recipe I use today satisfies my cravings, and it remains a favorite, it fails to align with my memories from Hawaii.

As mentioned at the start of this chapter, my time in Hawaii was cut short, mostly due to broken promises and my own naiveté. While I have no doubt that an extended stay would have revealed many more culinary wonders, and eventually the lifestyle that I craved, the few months spent on Oahu were entirely worthwhile. Although I returned to Los Angeles with a depleted bank account, and I endure a few emotional scars, I have absolutely no regrets.

# BEEF CHOW FUN
## Serves 4

---

*INGREDIENTS*

1 lb flank steak, thinly sliced across the grain
1 tablespoon corn starch
4 tablespoons light soy sauce, divided
1 lb rice noodles, extra wide
3 tablespoons peanut oil
4 cloves garlic, minced
1 tablespoon ginger, minced
2 tablespoons Shaoxing wine
1 teaspoon toasted sesame oil
1 tablespoon dark soy sauce
1/2 teaspoon sugar
1/2 cup green onions, cut into 1/2-inch lengths
2 cups mung bean shoots

*DIRECTIONS*

Mix the beef with the cornstarch and 1 tablespoon light soy sauce and let sit for 30 minutes.

Cook the noodles in boiling water for one minute, then remove from the heat. Let sit for five minutes, then drain.

Distribute the peanut oil over the bottom and sides of a wok over high heat. Add the garlic and ginger and toss, allowing to cook for 1 minute. Add the flank steak and toss until nearly done.

Add the wine, sesame oil, remaining light soy sauce, dark soy sauce and sugar, followed by the green onions, bean shoots and noodles, and toss until fully incorporated. Serve immediately.

# CHA CHIANG MEIN
## Serves 4

---

*INGREDIENTS*
2 tablespoons peanut oil
2 teaspoons garlic, chopped
2 tablespoons ginger, minced
3 tablespoons scallion, sliced coarsely
1 lb. minced pork
8 shitake mushrooms, finely chopped
3 tablespoons ground bean sauce
4 tablespoons hoisin sauce
2 tablespoons rice wine vinegar
1 tablespoon brown sugar
1 tablespoon sweet soy (kecap manis)
1/4 cup chicken stock
salt, to taste
1 lb. Chinese egg noodles
1/2 cucumber, seeded, then cut into matchstick strips

*DIRECTIONS*
Place wok over medium-high flame. Add the garlic, ginger and scallion and toss, cooking for about 1 minute. Add the pork followed by the mushrooms. Cook until the pork has browned.

Add the bean sauce, hoisin sauce, vinegar, sugar, sweet soy, and stock. Reduce the heat and cook for about 10 minutes. Add salt to taste. Remove from heat when fully cooked.

Prepare noodles according to directions until just tender, then drain. Toss with a little peanut oil to prevent sticking.

To serve, divide noodles equally into four bowls, top with meat sauce, then garnish with cucumber strips.

# HAR GOW (SHRIMP DUMPLINGS)
### Makes appx 24 dumplings

---

*INGREDIENTS*
1lb. shrimp, peeled, deveined, coarsely minced
1/2 cup water chestnuts, minced
2 scallions, minced (white part only)
1 tablespoon mirin
1 egg white
1 teaspoon soy sauce
1 teaspoon ginger, minced
1/2 teaspoon Asian sesame oil
1/2 teaspoon sugar
1/2 teaspoon salt
1/2 teaspoon pepper
2 tablespoons cornstarch
30 dim sum wrappers (Shanghai style)
water, for sealing the dumplings

*DIRECTIONS*
Combine the shrimp, water chestnuts, scallions, mirin, egg white, soy sauce, ginger, sesame oil, sugar, salt and pepper. Mix in the cornstarch, then let stand for 20 minutes.

Place a heaping teaspoon of the shrimp mixture in the center of a dim sum wrapper. Using your finger, wet the edges of the wrapper, then fold over and press together, forming a half circle dumpling. Place the completed dumpling on a tray, then repeat until all of the filling has been used.

To cook, line a bamboo steamer with a layer of lettuce leaves or parchment paper, place the dumplings on top, then steam for about 12 minutes. Serve immediately.

# SIU MAI - CHICKEN
## Makes about 20 dumplings

---

*INGREDIENTS*
1 lb. ground chicken (1/2 lb thigh, 1/2 lb breast)
1/2 cup water chestnuts, finely chopped
2 teaspoons ginger, finely minced
1 teaspoon garlic, finely minced
2 teaspoons oyster sauce
1/4 teaspoon Asian sesame oil
1/2 teaspoon salt
1/2 teaspoon black pepper
dim sum wrappers

*DIRECTIONS*
Combine the chicken, chestnuts, ginger, and garlic, followed by the oyster sauce, sesame oil, salt, and pepper.

Using a small spoon, scoop a little of the mixture and place in the center of a dumpling wrapper. Gather up the sides of the wrapper and pleat together around the filling, leaving the top open so the meat shows. Repeat, making more dim sum, until all of the filling has been used.

If desired, you can place the dumplings on a tray, cover and freeze. Once frozen, they can be transfered to a freezer bag for cooking at another time.

To prepare, line a bamboo steamer with a layer of lettuce leaves or parchment paper, place the dumplings on top, then steam for about 10 minutes. Serve immediately.

Serve with soy sauce, hot chili oil and/or hot Chinese mustard as condiments for dipping.

# SIU MAI - PORK
Makes about 30 dumplings

---

*INGREDIENTS*
1 lb. ground pork
1/2 cup water chestnuts, finely diced
1/2 cup shiitake mushrooms, chopped
1/4 cup scallions, finely chopped
1 tablespoon ginger, minced
2 teaspoons oyster sauce
1/4 teaspoon salt
1 tablespoon cornstarch
1/2 teaspoon Asian sesame oil
1 egg white, beaten
dim sum wrappers

*DIRECTIONS*
Combine the pork, mushrooms, water chestnuts, scallions and ginger followed by the oyster sauce, salt, cornstarch, soy sauce, sesame oil, and egg white. Mix thoroughly, making sure all of the ingredients are fully incorporated. Cover and refrigerate for at least 1 hour.

Using a small spoon, scoop a little of the mixture and place in the center of a dumpling wrapper. Gather up the sides of the wrapper and pleat together around the filling, leaving the top open so the meat shows. Repeat, making more dim sum, until all of the filling has been used.

To prepare, line a bamboo steamer with a layer of lettuce leaves or parchment paper, place the dumplings on top, then steam for about 10 minutes. Serve immediately.

# WONTON SOUP WITH NOODLES
## (Wor Wonton Gau Gee Mein)
Serves 8

---

*INGREDIENTS*

<u>Won Tons</u>

1 lb. ground pork

1/2 cup shiitake mushrooms, chopped

1/2 cup water chestnuts, finely diced

1/4 cup scallions, finely chopped

1 tablespoon ginger, minced

2 teaspoons oyster sauce

1/4 teaspoons salt

1 tablespoon cornstarch

1/2 teaspoons Asian sesame oil

1 egg white, beaten

dim sum wrappers

<u>Soup</u>

2 tablespoons peanut oil

1/4 cup scallions, thinly sliced

1/4 cup Shitake (dried) mushrooms, restored and thinly sliced

2 tablespoons ginger, finely minced

6 cups chicken stock

2 teaspoons soy sauce

1 teaspoon rice wine vinegar

salt, to taste

4 oz. spinach leaves

1 lb. Chinese egg noodles, fresh

*DIRECTIONS*

Mix together the pork, mushrooms, water chestnuts, scallions and ginger followed by the oyster sauce, salt, cornstarch, soy sauce, sesame oil, and egg white. Mix thoroughly, making sure all of the ingredients are fully incorporated. Cover and refrigerate for at least 1 hour.

To assemble, place a heaping teaspoon of the meat mixture onto the center of a wonton wrapper. Using your finger, wet the edges of the wrapper with water, then fold over and pinch closed, creating a half circle shaped dumpling.

Continue making the dumplings until all of the filling is used up. If using right away, simply cover with a moist cloth and set aside. If preparing in advance, wontons can be frozen and used straight from the freezer, as needed.

To make the soup, pour the oil into the bottom of a large soup pot over medium high heat. Add the scallions, mushrooms and garlic and cook for 2 minutes. Add the stock and bring to a boil. Reduce to a simmer, add the soy, vinegar, salt and spinach and cook for 15 minutes.

Bring a separate pot of water to a boil and cook the noodles, per directions on the package.

As soon as the noodles are ready, add the wontons to the simmering soup. Continue cooking, gently stirring, until the wontons are cooked through, approximately 6 minutes.

Place an equal amount of noodles in 8 individual serving bowls. Cover the noodles with soup and few wontons. Serve immediately.

 Cooking classes would allow me to expand my culinary vocabulary beyond mac-n-cheese and store bought spaghetti.

**M**y encounters with Australia took place on three separate occasions and were pivotal to my ability to appreciate and prepare good food. My first visit took place in the early 1980's, a time when air travel was expensive, the country was far too remote for most Americans, and it took way too long to get there. International business communication was still being handled via teletype, the most commonly utilized handheld technology was the pocket calculator, and it was well before "Crocodile Dundee" (released in September 1986) became a worldwide cinematic sensation. A second trip would be organized a year later and the third, which included a romantic encounter and marriage, would take place about 10 years thereafter. Let's start from the top.

Having been curious about Australia for a while, I learned that Qantas Airways was offering significantly reduced fares.

Having recently completed a sizable commission with a fat paycheck, the timing could not have been better. I booked a flight, picked up a guidebook, packed my bags, and headed off for the Antipodes.

My agenda included a week-long visit in Melbourne followed by another week in Sydney, the two most densely populated and frequently visited cities on the continent.

During this time, I made the effort to visit all of the typical tourist destinations - art museums, parks and gardens, historic landmarks, zoos, etc. In Melbourne, I would marvel at the clocks on the facade of Flinders Street train station, enjoy one of the oldest roller-coasters in the world operating within Luna Park, and take leisurely strolls along the Yarra River. In Sydney, I would make a point to visit all of the attractions in Sydney Harbor, take a ferry to Manly, and check out the nightlife in Kings Cross.

Along the way, I would fall in love with the iconic Four'N Twenty meat pie. Sold throughout Australia in milk bars (convenience stores), sidewalk food stands, and fast casual restaurants, these tasty pastries, filled with beef, mutton and carrots, remain standard fare, even today. In addition, having noticed lots of places displaying barrel-sized cones of meat slowly roasting on an open spit, I would discover the Greek gyro - a pita bread filled with thinly shaved strips of lamb accompanied by lettuce, tomato, hummus, tzatziki and a drizzle of harissa hot sauce.

While in Sydney, I discovered Harry's Cafe de Wheels, a re-nowned pie cart located near the gates of the Wooloomooloo naval yard (it took me a while to pronounce this - somewhat like "skip-to-my-lou"). Deciphering its extensive list of meat pies, I selected the "Tiger's Eye," a chunky beef pie topped with mashed potatoes, mushy peas, and gravy. To my tremendous delight, when it came to late night snacks, it wouldn't get any better than this.

Considering that my culinary preferences had not yet evolved beyond mac-n-cheese, and my focus was taking in the remarkable sights and sounds that only Australia could offer, it's not surprising that my recall is limited to these few savory treats.

What was truly noteworthy, along with the spectacular flora and fauna I encountered throughout the country, was the feeling of having entered a time warp, going back to the mid-1950s and a far simpler existence. In particular, I enjoyed the relaxed tempo of everyday living, the rustic corner pubs where locals gathered on a regular basis, and the quaint little milk bars that stocked everything from milk, candy, and newspapers, to toiletries, canned foods, and laundry detergent. Best still, they served meat pies from a heated display bearing the Four'N Twenty logo. Needless to say, I patronized more than my fair share of milk bars.

After returning home, and over the course of the following year, I became increasingly eager to continue my Australian adventure. Learning that reduced fares were still available, I purchased another ticket and headed back to Oz (slang for Australia). This time around, my agenda focused on Queensland (Australia's tropical north) and the Great Barrier Reef.

Arriving in Sydney, I quickly secured a rental car and managed to drive out of the city without inflicting injury (this would be the first time driving on the left side of the street using a steering wheel on the right side of the car). Setting a north-bound course following along the coast highway, I was heading towards the places that my guide book and a few friends had recommended - Noosa Heads (a small beach resort community), Heron Island (the southern most outcropping of the Great Barrier Reef), Port Douglas (a rustic holiday destination for deep sea fishing, diving and snorkeling), and Kakadu National Park (Australia's largest national park - renown for its natural beauty, bio-diversity and ancient cultural heritage).

The drive from Sydney to Noosa Heads was significantly longer than expected. What I failed to realize is just how big the Australian continent was and how much time it would take to drive from one point to another. The good news was all the charming small towns I'd encounter along the way, including friendly corner pubs and amply stocked milk bars, all catering to my cravings for Four'N Twenty meat pies. No worries!

Noosa Heads was a delightful beach community just north of Brisbane along the Queensland coast. It was the perfect place to relax, have a few drinks, meet some locals, hang on the beach, and enjoy the sunshine. What I could not know is that Noosa would expose me to the laugh of a kookaburra and introduce me to a local delicacy that would become my all time favorite shellfish, surpassing my love of Maryland blue crabs and Maine lobster.

Let's just say that the laugh of a kookaburra is contagious. From the very first time in Noosa, and every time thereafter, this native kingfisher's distinctive warble would always, and still does, bring a smile to my face. Of course, if I made a fuss about this remarkable bird, the Aussies simply wrote me off as a crazy American tourist.

The shellfish that caught my attention was described as "bugs." Since I could not resist such an unusual offering, I inquired further. While they do have a bit of a creepy-crawly appearance, they are not bugs or insects at all. They are a variety of slipper lobster called Moreton Bay Bugs harvested from, and named after, the bay that hugs Brisbane's eastern coast.

No matter where I was, and whether they were steamed, sautéed, grilled, or baked into a casserole, I'd indulge. Even when they were being offered from a makeshift seafood stand on the side of the road, I'd pull over and buy a few. There's nothing like cruising the coast of Australia while munching away on freshly steamed bugs.

My next stop was Heron Island, a coral outcropping on the southernmost tip of the Great Barrier Reef that could only be accessed via helicopter or ferry. Known for its astonishing natural beauty, I took the time to experience it all.

While the food on Heron was unremarkable, the Aussies introduced me to Port as an easy to drink beverage after dinner. I came to regard Port, along with other varieties of fortified wines generally referred to as "sticky," as a highly enjoyable accompaniment to whatever cake, pudding, or other such dessert was being served. Being young and carefree, and in rollicking good company, one glass would lead to another, and another... I'm sure you get the drift.

Once I had recovered from my adventures on Heron Island, it was back in the car and farther northward along the coast highway, past Cairns, and into the sleepy tropical town of Port Douglas. While its roads, marina and hotels have been spruced up over the years, at the time of my visit, it was still a rustic and well-worn place reminiscent of the small towns that appeared in 50's era cowboy films. While I do not remember much (could have been the volume of Port I consumed), I have very fond memories of Mocka's Pies & Bakehouse.

Mocka's, a Port Douglas tradition since 1969, was a small bakery specializing in beef, steak, and chicken pies. Made by hand, these were significantly better than the commercially available varieties, immediately apparent with just one bite.

Apparently, I am not the only one who has fallen in love with Mocka's pies. Research indicates the bakery has expanded over the years - now serving up pies with more exotic and esoteric fillings including Tuna Mornay, Green Curry Chicken, Curry Beef, Pumpkin Spinach & Feta, Crocodile, and Kangaroo. Their seafood pie, filled with wild caught barramundi, scallops and prawns, is a house specialty. Were I to visit Port Douglas today, you'd better believe I'd make a bee-line to the place and order up several of those little beauties.

The last adventure on this particular trek included a few days in the Northern Territory exploring Kakadu National Park as well as the city of Darwin on Australia's northernmost coast off the Timor Sea. While I found Kakadu's flora and fauna exceptional, and I had lots of enjoyable experiences in Darwin, I'll simply recommend that you take a trip and see for yourself. From a culinary perspective, the best part was the introduction to farmed barramundi and beefalo.

As part of an organized tour to Kakadu, we were taken to one of the smaller ranches in the Northern Territory where commercial farming of Barramundi (Asian Sea Bass) was starting up. Native to Australia and the Indo-Pacific, this lean, lightly flavored, and meaty fish was virtually unknown in the United States. Caught fresh and grilled, this was one of the most delicious fin fish experiences I'd ever had. I continue to enjoy barramundi today, whenever and wherever I can find it.

This same rancher also raised animals that were a hybrid of cattle and bison. The resulting beefalo, served to us as a grilled burger alongside the fish, was absolutely amazing. Lean, flavorful and tender, everything you might want from a burger and more. Sadly, this is the only time I've been served beefalo and have not found it on menus since. That being said, it was one of the best damned burgers I've ever had. Coupled with the barramundi, this particular meal remains a treasured culinary memory and part of the enduring fondness I have for the land down-under.

My third encounter with Oz took place about ten years later, including a residency that would last for eight years. It was during this time that I took considerably greater interest in food and would sign up for cooking classes.

For this trip, I would be living in Melbourne with the Australian woman who, 14 years later, would become my ex-wife. Since I did not have residency, was not allowed to work (it would take a year to acquire legal residency) finances were limited, and we could not afford to eat out, I decided that cooking classes would allow me to expand my culinary vocabulary beyond mac-n-cheese and store bought spaghetti.

It's important to note that, as part of the Pacific Rim, Australia has a large number of ethnic populations that includes Korean, Malaysian, Thai, Indian, and Chinese. Accordingly, many of the foods we preferred were linked to these cultures.

It goes without saying, the inexpensive and widely available Australian street foods including meat pies, gyros, sausage rolls (sausage meat wrapped in pastry), and chicken schnitzels (pounded thin, breaded and fried) would become dietary standards while out and about. What we ate at home, however, would be significantly influenced by two television personalities - Chef Ian Hewitson and Chef Gabriel Gaté.

Hewitson (Huey as he is affectionately known) would host the culinary segments that were part of the immensely popular lifestyle-oriented show "Healthy Wealthy and Wise." Whether he was cooking up something special, visiting restaurants, or extolling the virtues of specific Australian ingredients, this would be one of the ways I started to increase my culinary vocabulary.

Chef Gabriel Gaté also appeared on equally well-known and highly-regarded lifestyle show and operated a culinary school not terribly far from where I lived in Melbourne. With time on my hands, I enrolled in his classes, building a foundation upon which my culinary skills would blossom.

One of the most noteworthy dishes I learned was Char Kway Teow. This popular Malaysian stir fry, made with fish cake, shrimp, crab, sambal oelek (chili sauce), and wide rice noodles, has become one of my perennial favorites.

The same instructor would also teach us how to make Maryland Crab Cakes. Before starting, knowing that Marylanders are fussy about their beloved crab cakes, she asked if anyone was from Maryland. When I raised my hand, she admitted I would not like her recipe. She was right.

My exposure to Malaysian, Indonesian and Thai foods was enhanced by repeated visits to Chinta Ria, a charming

Malaysian restaurant situated just off Lygon Street in the Carlton neighborhood. Operated by Chef Simon Goh, I was won over by his Nasi Lemak (a coconut rice dish), Roti Canai (a soft and flaky flatbread served with a curry sauce), Curry Laksa (chicken and coconut based soup with noodles), and Hokkien Mee (stir fried noodles). His peanut sauce, served as an accompaniment to Satay (skewered and grilled meats) was to die for.

When Chef Goh published his first cookbook, he included recipes for Curry Laksa, Tod Mun Pla (Thai Fish Cakes), and his famed Peanut Sauce. While they did not quite match up to what had been served in the restaurant, I was able to modify them to suit my preferences.

I started buying other cookbooks that featured Asian cuisines as well, some easier to follow than others. Most notable was Charmaine Solomon's "The Complete Asian Cookbook." Using this book, I developed a fluency with dishes that were common throughout Thailand, Indonesia, and Malaysia as well as a few richly fragrant curries from India. If you are interested in Asian cooking, I highly recommend any of the books that she's written.

One of my more meaningful chef encounters was Chef Michael Bacash, owner of Toofey's, considered Melbourne's premier seafood restaurant at that time (while the name Toofey's endures, apparently Chef Bacash has moved on to open a different restaurant in South Yarra). While his preparation of simply grilled seafood was exquisite, he made a heavenly Seafood Risotto that I would order time and time again.

It wasn't until Chef Bacash appeared on television and disclosed his recipe that I discovered his magic touch. Aside from using the best possible ingredients, it seems the dish requires a full pound of butter. Considering this is a recipe for four, and one stick of butter per person seems a tad obscene, I nudged it towards more healthful proportions. While I learned to make other risottos over time, this version featuring shrimp, scallops, calamari, and spinach is by far the best.

I also learned that having access to fresh, flavorful, and high quality ingredients is essential. In Melbourne, this meant shopping at one of the three traditional markets that were closest to my home in South Melbourne. While Prahran Market was my favorite for the absolute best in fresh produce, meats, seafood and specialty foods, the Queen Victoria and South Melbourne markets were also quite good.

The best part of shopping in these places was getting to know the traders, discovering their specialties, building familiarity, and establishing trust. If they weren't too busy, they would always point out something new or particularly worthwhile. When there were items I had never seen or tasted, they would take extra time to explain how they could be incorporated into recipes and the impact they would have.

While each of these markets had its own distinctive personality and housed a noticeably different assortment of vendors - from green grocers and fish mongers to purveyors of smallgoods and confectionery, anything you might need could be found. Knowing that each market had vendors who specialized in ready-to-eat foods, it was dangerous to arrive hungry. That being said, and if I was in the mood, I would always grab a coffee and a snack before or after making the rounds.

# AUSSIE MEAT PIE
Serves 4

---

*INGREDIENTS*
<u>Filling</u>
1 tablespoon olive oil
1 1/2 cups onions, finely chopped
4 cloves garlic, minced
3/4 lb. ground beef
3/4 lb. ground pork
3/4 cup chicken stock
3 tablespoons flour
6 oz. tomato paste
1 tablespoon Worcestershire sauce
1 tablespoon soy sauce
1 teaspoon celery seed
1/2 teaspoon black pepper
salt, to taste

<u>Pastry</u>
1 1/4 cups flour
1 teaspoon salt
1 stick butter, cold, cut into small pieces
3 tablespoons milk, divided
1 egg

*DIRECTIONS*
Preheat the oven to 425°F.

<u>To make the filling:</u> Heat the oil in a saucepan over medium high heat. Add the onion and garlic, cooking for 3 minutes until soft. Add the beef and pork and cook for 5-10 minutes until browned, taking care to break up large clumps of meat.

Mix the flour and 1/4 cup stock to form a paste and set aside.

Add the remaining stock, tomato paste, Worcestershire, soy sauce, celery seed, and pepper to the meat and stir until fully incorporated. Bring the meat to a boil, then reduce heat to medium-low. Simmer for 10 minutes until almost dry, then stir in the flour mixture. Continue cooking until thickened, add salt as needed, then remove from heat and allow to cool.

To make the pastry: Mix the flour and salt in a food processor. Gradually pulse in the butter until the mixture becomes granular, then pulse in 2 tablespoons of milk, a little at a time, to make a dough.

Roll the dough on a floured board to a 1/8" thickness. Cut into four, 6-inch, rounds.

To assemble: Spoon equal amounts of filling into four, 4-inch diameter ramekins. Top with pastry, tucking under the edges to make a thick crust around the rim. Press the edges with a fork to create a tight seal against the edge of the ramekin.

Beat the egg and the remaining 1 tablespoon milk together. Brush the top of each pastry with the egg wash, then bake for approximately 25 minutes until golden brown.

Serve with "Dead Horse" (Australian slang for ketchup).

# CHAR KWAY TEOW
## Serves 4

---

INGREDIENTS

3 tablespoons peanut oil
3 teaspoons garlic, minced
4 oz. fish cake,* thinly sliced
8 shrimp, cleaned
4 oz. crab meat
8 oz. wide rice noodles, fresh (or dry rice stick noodles - the cooked weight should be 8oz.)
2 tablespoons mushroom soy sauce
2 tablespoons light soy sauce
2 teaspoons sambal oelek*
1 egg, beaten
1/4 teaspoon white pepper
4 oz. bean shoots
1 tablespoon garlic chives,* thinly sliced

DIRECTIONS

This is a fast moving dish. Accordingly, you'll want to be sure to have all of your ingredients fully prepared, measured and standing by prior to cooking. In professional kitchens, this is referred to as "mise en place," the French term meaning "everything is ready and in place."

Pour the oil into a wok and heat until shimmering. Working quickly, add the garlic and toss briefly. Add the fish cake, shrimp and crab and toss. When just cooked, add in the noodles, mushroom soy, regular soy and sambal. If the noodles get dry, toss in a little water to keep things from sticking.

Move the noodles off to the sides, opening up the center of

the wok. Add the egg, sprinkle with pepper and scramble together. As soon as the egg begins to set, break apart and toss all of the ingredients together.

Divide the Kway Teow into four bowls, then garnish with bean shoots and chives.

NOTE: You may want to place extra soy sauce and sambal on the table so that the Kway Teow can be adjusted to personal taste preferences.

*Available in most Asian supermarkets.

---

*"I'm not a doctor but I know adding cheese to anything makes it an antidepressant."*
*Unknown*

---

# CURRY LAKSA
Serves 4

---

*INGREDIENTS*

*The Paste*

1 onion, coarsely chopped

1 tablespoon ginger, coarsely chopped

1 tablespoon galangal, coarsely chopped

2 garlic cloves, coarsely chopped

2 stalks lemongrass, coarsely chopped

2 dried birdseye chilies, coarsely chopped

4 macadamia nuts

1 tablespoon blanchan (shrimp paste)

*The Soup*

3 tablespoons peanut oil

1 teaspoon ground coriander

1 teaspoon sweet paprika

1 teaspoon turmeric

1 teaspoon ground cumin

2 cups coconut milk

3 cups chicken stock

1 teaspoon sugar

1 teaspoon salt

*The Assembly*

1/2 lb. Hokkien egg noodle, cooked

1/2 lb. vermicelli rice stick, cooked

16 shrimp, large, fully cooked

1 cup shredded chicken breast, fully cooked

1 cup bean sprouts

16 green beans, fully cooked

8 squares beancurd puff, cut diagonally into triangles

*DIRECTIONS*

To make the soup, start by making the paste. Place the onion, ginger, galangal, garlic, lemongrass, chilies, nuts and blanchan in a blender, processing to form a fine paste. You can add a drizzle of oil or chicken stock if needed to loosen everything up.

You are now ready to make the soup. Pour the oil into a 6-quart casserole over medium-high heat. Fry the paste for 5 minutes until fragrant, taking care not to burn. Add the coriander, paprika, turmeric and cumin and continue frying for 2 more minutes. Add the coconut milk, stock, sugar and salt, and bring to a boil. Once boiled, check the soup for flavor, adjusting the sugar and/or salt, as needed. Once the flavor is balanced, reduce the heat and keep warm until ready to serve.

Place equal amounts of the egg noodle and rice stick in each of four bowls, then arrange equal amounts of shrimp, chicken, green beans, bean sprouts and beancurd puff triangles.

Slowly ladle equal portions of the hot soup into each of the four bowls. Serve immediately.

# SEAFOOD RISOTTO
Serves 4

---

*INGREDIENTS*
1 cup arborio rice
1/2 medium onion - chopped
2 cloves garlic - crushed
2 tablespoons olive oil
4 bay leaves
2 cups fish stock
1/4 cup white wine
16 large shrimp (shelled)
12 scallops
1/4 lb. calamari
1/4 lb. fresh baby spinach
4 tablespoons butter
1/2 cup grated Parmesan
salt and pepper to taste

*DIRECTIONS*
In a small saucepan, bring stock to a boil and reduce to simmer.

Heat the oil in a larger pot. Add the onions, bay leaves and garlic and sauté until soft. Add the rice and stir for one minute.

Using low heat, stir in the stock, a little at a time until it has been fully absorbed. Add the wine and continue stirring until it is fully absorbed. Add more wine, stock or water, as needed, to reach the desired consistency and flavor.

Fold in the shrimp, scallops, calamari and spinach and cover. Seafood will be adequately cooked in 3 - 5 minutes. Gently fold in the butter and cheese, taking care not to break apart the seafood. Add salt and pepper to taste. Serve immediately.

# THAI FISH CAKES
### Serves 6

___

INGREDIENTS
2 lb. red snapper fillets
2 eggs, beaten
4 tablespoons red curry paste
1 lime leaf, finely chopped
2 tablespoons fresh cilantro
2 teaspoons sugar
1/2 teaspoon salt
peanut oil for frying

DIRECTIONS
Steam the fish. When fully cooked, transfer to a bowl and cool.
Break up the cooled fish into a coarse crumble.

In a large bowl, whisk together the eggs, curry paste, lime leaf,
cilantro, sugar, and salt. Gently fold in the fish, maintaining its
coarse texture. Form the mixture into 12 equally sized balls,
than press into patties.

Pour a 1/4 inch layer of oil into a straight-walled sauté pan.
Using medium-high heat, fry the fish cakes, turning after
browned on one side. When browned on both sides, place
the fish cakes on paper towels to absorb any remaining oil.

Repeat this process until all of the fish cakes are cooked. You
may need to top up the oil along the way.

Serve on a bed of jasmine rice with peanut sauce or sweet chili
sauce.*

* Sweet chili sauce is available in Asian grocery stores as well as
most supermarkets with a well-stocked international aisle.

# THAI PEANUT SAUCE
Makes about 2 cups

---

*INGREDIENTS*
1/2 cup onion, coarsely chopped
1 tablespoon garlic, coarsely chopped
1 tablespoon ginger, coarsely chopped
1 birdseye chili, coarsely chopped
1 stalk lemongrass, coarsely chopped
1 tablespoon peanut oil
8 oz. peanut butter
1/2 cup tamarind juice*
1 tablespoon brown sugar
1 tablespoon kecap menis (sweet soy)
1 lemon, juiced

*DIRECTIONS*
Place the onion, garlic, ginger, chili, and lemongrass in a blender and purée, until completely smooth. Add a little water, if needed, to loosen.

Place the oil in a 2-quart sauce pan. Add the purée and fry over medium high heat for 2 minutes until fragrant. Stir in the peanut butter, tamarind juice, brown sugar, kecap menis, and lemon juice. Add salt, to taste.

*Tamarind pulp is available at most Asian grocery stores. To make a juice, mash a 1 inch lump of pulp into 1/2 C boiling water. Once the pulp has softened and a juice has formed, strain out the solids, then use the juice, as needed.

**Washington, DC**

The number one culinary encounter that took place in DC was almost as memorable as losing my virginity.

**A**t the ripe age of 24, I decided that having a west coast office in Santa Monica during winter months and an east coast office during the summer would increase the number of business opportunities I could exploit and, at the same time, allow me to enjoy warmer weather on a year-round basis.

To test this idea, I sublet my Santa Monica apartment, packed up a few essentials, and moved to the cool and groovy neighborhood of Dupont Circle in Washington DC. In the 80s, this was a neighborhood in transition, bordered by well-regarded neighborhoods to the north, south and west, and a less than salubrious neighborhood to the east.

To further set the scene, disco was all the rage, making the alternative lifestyle clubs the cultural center of the universe among the young and beautiful urbanites. Cocaine was just beginning to gain popularity, complementing poppers (amyl nitrate), pot and Quaaludes as the party favors of choice among the young and naively invincible. George H.W. Bush (41) was in office, John Travolta was the box office sensation and, aside from the relatively small number of individuals who considered their mouth a major pleasure organ, there was not much said about food other than "What's for dinner?" or "Did you make reservations?"

Having learned to appreciate restaurants during my childhood years in Baltimore, and then again in Los Angeles where my circle of friends supped among the social elite every time a new restaurant opened its doors, I was on the lookout for new and different culinary adventures in our nation's capital. Considering my priorities aligned primarily with sex, drugs and rock-n-roll, I found my circle of friends in DC were nowhere near as interested in food as were those in Southern California. Needless to say, my culinary experiences in D.C. aligned more with the late-night spots we gravitated towards that would provide a fast, tasty (and usually greasy) antidote to the abundance of alcohol that we consumed on a regular basis.

For whatever reason, my time in Washington never included a visit to Ben's Chili Bowl. Today, it is considered one of D.C.'s culinary landmarks, renowned for its Chili Con Carne, Chili Dogs and Chili Burgers. Considering the fascination I had with similar fare in L.A., how this escaped my attention is a mystery.

I did, however, take a fancy to the chili dogs that were served from the ubiquitous hot dog carts that would position themselves at key intersections around town. It was during these late-night rendezvous that I would learn about D.C.'s local sausage delicacy - the Half Smoke.

Truth be told, I found little difference, other than texture and a touch of spice, between the half smoke and the hot dog, especially when it's been drowned in chili, onions and mustard. Regardless, they were a wonderful snack, especially at 2:00am just after the bars had closed their doors.

When it came to late night fare, my favorites were served up nightly at Trio's, a stalwart D.C. institution that, back in those days, would keep its doors open to revelers until 3:00am. This is the place that, for me, set the standard for the all-time best meatball sub ever. We're talking about an oversized submarine roll stuffed with meatballs, topped with an Italian red sauce and handfuls of grated mozzarella, all placed under the broiler to achieve toasty perfection. At that time, and at that hour, with a persisting buzz from the night's not yet concluded activities, Trio's was the place to be and their subs were the undeniable champions of late night gastronomy.

As a matter of clarification, my meals were not always fast, fried, and greasy affairs that took place after the majority of Washingtonians had gone to bed. In fact, many were enjoyed during traditional dinnertime hours at very reputable restaurants and rank among my most treasured dining memories.

The number one culinary encounter that took place in DC was almost as memorable as losing my virginity. My newfound girlfriend and I decided to splurge on a meal at one of the more acclaimed restaurants on Connecticut Avenue. While I cannot remember its name (I remember hers - Terry - we have remained friends for nearly 40 years), I recall the romantic lighting, tight spaces, small tables, and efficient service. The defining moment, however, was my discovery of this incredibly dark, intensely rich, unbelievably dense, perfectly sweet, and nearly orgasmic slice of wonderfulness called Flourless Chocolate Cake. While I have found other desserts to be incredibly satisfying and enjoyable, and there are savory foods that I've encountered that are equally memorable and noteworthy, no other confection has surpassed this one.

In the wake of this encounter, it became my life's ambition to find a recipe for the penultimate chocolate cake, flourless or otherwise. While working my way through a seemingly endless number of cookbooks and baking magazines, it became clear that my obsession might take some time. Along the way, however, I learned how to handle chocolate, make ganache, distinguish between the rich and wonderful qualities of Valrhona (from France), Callebaut (from Belgium) and Ibarra (from Mexico), and fully appreciate the difference between milk, semi-sweet, dark and white varieties. While there were unavoidable failures, I have successfully developed recipes for both flourless and traditional chocolate cakes that continue to win praise from highly discriminating chocoholics.

Around this same time, I had my first encounter with Larimer's, a food lover's paradise in the middle of the city and just a few blocks away from my apartment. This small, yet perfectly stocked boutique introduced the community to some of the most esoteric, exotic, and undeniably delicious foods from every corner of the planet. While they maintained impressive selections of wine, kitchenware, and shelf stable delights, my favorite part of the store was their cheese counter.

To put this in perspective, my experience with cheese had been pretty much limited to American slices wrapped in plastic, supermarket cheddar, grated Parmesan in a green can, and Philadelphia cream cheese. While I never fussed over their labels, I recall "cheese food" identified as a primary ingredient.

I'm still not entirely sure what that means but, as that time, ignorance was bliss.

Needless to say, the cheeses that Larimer's offered were significantly better in terms of quality, texture, aroma, and flavor. While brie, camembert and bleu represented a challenge to my immature palate, it was the bold, tangy flavor of imported and aged cheddar and gouda that got my attention, especially Double Gloucester with Chives.

It was obvious that the staff at Larimer's took great pleasure in their work. I learned about Red Dragon, Red Leicester, and soon realized that just about any flavor forward, yellow cheese imported from England or Holland would float my boat. Of course, my vocabulary has expanded over the years and I've become a vocal advocate for cheeses including Grafton Village, Collier's, Prima Donna, Beecher's and Neal's Yard to name a few. That being said, if there's a reputable Double Gloucester with Chives in the cheese case, that's what I'll buy.

Larimer's also introduced me to Carr's Table Water Crackers. They patiently informed me that, when it comes to crackers, there's more to life than Ritz, Saltines and Wheat Thins.

Clearly, the time I spent in our nation's capital as a young man was a culinary coming of age. Since then, I have returned on many occasions, always making time to check out some of the latest and greatest restaurants and innovative ethnic operations that have been popping up all over town.

While these investigations are always enjoyable (including the occasional half smoke from a hot dog cart), there are two recent encounters that have made indelible impressions.

If you've driven in and around DC any time in the last few

years, you know that traffic is a never ending battle, especially on the freeways that connect the city with outlying suburbs. For this reason, and whether I drive into town or take public transportation, I always leave plenty of time for unexpected delays. I also make sure to bring a book so that, should I arrive way too early, I can go to a nearby deli, cafe, or restaurant and pass the time over a cup of coffee and/or snack.

On one of my most recent visits, traffic and parking were surprisingly cooperative, allowing me to reach my destination 90 minutes ahead of schedule. With book in hand, I went in search of coffee. Since my meeting was taking place in the heart of the city, there were plenty of options including bakeries, coffee shops, ethnic restaurants, and fast casual options. The place that got my attention bore the name "Melt Shop."

As you may have already noticed, cheese is one of my all-time favorite foods. Whether it has been sliced from a wedge, oozes from a grilled sandwich, or is the key ingredient that transforms a culinary masterpiece, cheese is always a welcome treat. Assuming the word "melt" implied an emphasis on cheese, I was compelled to investigate further.

As expected, this was one of those trendy grilled cheese places that responded to the popularity of comfort foods. The menu at Melt Shop was impressive - listing concoctions of every size, shape and description featuring all sorts of thick, melting, and gooey cheeses. Since I was anticipating a lunch meeting, and not feeling all that gluttonous, I limited my selection to a relatively small and manageable side dish of Tater Tots.

Let's just say these were not your ordinary tots. While the little fried balls of grated potato were predictable, they came to life under a blanket of cheese sauce, grated Parmesan, pickled jalapeno peppers and crumbled bacon. I was in L - O - V - E. Of course, I took copious notes, a few photos, and made it an immediate task to replicate this dish at home.

With tried and true recipes for potato pancakes and cheese sauce already in my repertoire, it did not take long before I had come up with my own version of this delightfully cheesy treat. Ranking right up there with chili fries, chili mac, poutine, and mac-n-cheese, I call this dish "Tots with the Lot."

By comparison, my other culinary encounter was relatively tame - basically a new way of looking at an old favorite - potato salad. For decades, the only potato salads I had ever had were all mayonnaise based with slight variations based on inclusions (yellow mustard, wasabi, ground mustard powder, sour cream, sweet pickle relish, finely chopped red capsicum, crumbled hard boiled eggs, chopped dill, grated ginger) as well as the way the potatoes were prepared (skin on, peeled, sliced, small chunks, large chunks).

On this particular day, I enjoyed a chunky potato salad made with a basic vinaigrette that was absolutely delicious. While there is nothing terribly complicated about this recipe, and it falls well below the stature of Flourless Chocolate Cake, Double Gloucester with Chives and Tots with the Lot, the combination of olive oil, cider vinegar, and coarse-grain Dijon mustard tossed into a bowl of firm, cooked potatoes was remarkably enjoyable. While my love affair with mayonnaise endures, and mayo-based potato salads are still my favorites, I make this recipe every now and then as a delightful and refreshing break from tradition.

# AMY'S POTATO SALAD
### Serves 8 - 10

_____

*INGREDIENTS*
4 lb. red potatoes
4 tablespoons white wine vinegar
2 tablespoons coarse dijon mustard
2 tablespoon olive oil
2 teaspoons sugar
salt and pepper, to taste

*DIRECTIONS*
Clean the potatoes, removing any eyes, unwanted blemishes, or grit, then cut into large dice and place in a stock pot.

Cover the potatoes with water and bring to a boil. Once boiling, continue cooking for about 10 minutes. When the potatoes are just tender, remove from the heat, transfer to a colander, rinse in cold water several times, and allow to drain.

In the meantime, using a large bowl, whisk together the vinegar, mustard, oil, sugar, salt and pepper. Adjust for taste, as needed.

Carefully fold the potatoes in with the dressing. When fully mixed, refrigerate for 3 hours.

After 3 hours, toss the potato salad once again, adjust the seasoning, as needed, and refrigerate for an additional 3 hours or overnight.

Toss the potatoes once again, just before serving.

# FLOURLESS CHOCOLATE CAKE
Serves 10

---

*INGREDIENTS*
1/3 cup water
1/2 cup sugar
1/2 cup butter, cut into chunks
12 oz. dark chocolate, coarsely chopped
1/3 cup Cointreau, or good quality orange liqueur
6 eggs, beaten
whipped cream, for garnish
fresh raspberries or sliced strawberries, for garnish

*DIRECTIONS*
Grease the sides and bottom of an 8" spring-form pan with butter, then cover these surfaces with parchment paper.

Preheat the oven to 350°F.

Bring the water and sugar to a boil, stirring until the sugar is fully dissolved. Remove from the heat, then stir in the butter and chocolate, making sure the butter and chocolate are completely melted and a smooth texture is achieved.

Whisk in the Cointreau, followed by the eggs, then pour the mixture into the prepared spring-form pan.

Place the cake pan in a larger baking tray, filling the outer tray with enough water so that it comes half way up the cake pan. Bake for 45 minutes or until the center of the cake is set.

Remove from the oven and cool thoroughly before serving.

To serve, cut into thin slices, then garnish with whipped cream and fresh berries.

# IBARRA CHOCOLATE CAKE
## Serves 10

---

*INGREDIENTS*
4 oz. butter
6 oz. bittersweet chocolate
6 oz. Ibarra chocolate
2 egg yolks
1/2 cup sugar
1 teaspoon vanilla extract
1/2 teaspoon salt
1/2 cup flour
8 egg whites

*DIRECTIONS*
Preheat the oven to 375°F.

Grease a 9" spring-form pan with butter, then line the bottom and sides with parchment paper.

Using a double boiler, melt the butter and two chocolates.

In a large bowl, whisk together the yolks, sugar, vanilla and salt. Slowly add the chocolate and flour, alternating each, until all of the ingredients are combined.

Beat the egg whites until stiff and fluffy. Gently fold into the chocolate mixture, a little at a time, until fully incorporated.

Pour the batter into the prepared cake pan, then bake for approximately 35 minutes, until the center of the cake is firm.

Remove from oven and cool completely before serving.

To serve, dust cake slices with confectioner's sugar along with a spoonful of whipped cream.

# MEATBALL SUBS
Serves 8

---

*INGREDIENTS*

<u>Meatballs</u> (makes 48 meatballs)

2 tablespoons olive oil

2 cups onion, finely chopped

1 tablespoon garlic, minced

1/2 cup breadcrumbs

2 eggs

3/4 cup Parmesan cheese, grated

1/2 cup flat leaf parsley, chopped

1/2 cup fresh basil, chopped

1 teaspoon oregano, dried

2 teaspoons salt

1 teaspoon pepper

1 lb. ground beef

1 lb. ground pork

<u>Sauce</u>

2 tablespoons olive oil

1 tablespoon garlic, minced

1 1/2 cups onions, finely chopped

1 red capsicum, cut into very thin strips

28 oz. crushed tomatoes (canned)

1 cup dry white wine

1/4 cup fresh basil, finely chopped

1 teaspoon crushed red pepper

1 teaspoon marjoram

1/2 teaspoon salt

<u>Submarine</u>
8 8-inch submarine rolls
1 cup Parmesan, grated
2 cups mozzarella, grated

*DIRECTIONS*
Preheat the oven to 350°F.

<u>To make the meatballs</u>: Sauté the onion and garlic until soft, about 5 minutes, then transfer to large mixing bowl. Add the breadcrumbs, eggs, Parmesan, parsley, basil, oregano, salt and pepper and mix thoroughly. Using your hands, mix in the beef and pork until fully incorporated.

Using a level measure from a 1 1/2 inch ice cream scoop, form equal amounts of the meat mixture into balls and arrange onto a 13 inch x 18 inch baking sheet (you should be able to fit 8 rows of 6 meatballs each).

Bake the meatballs for 15 minutes, turn once, and continue baking for another 10 minutes. Once the meatballs are nicely browned, remove from oven and set aside.

<u>To make the sauce</u>: Place the olive oil in a large saucepan over medium-high heat. Stir in the garlic, onions and capsicum and sauté for 10 minutes, allowing the vegetables to soften.

Stir in the crushed tomatoes, wine, basil, crushed red pepper, marjoram, and salt. Bring the sauce to a boil, then reduce to simmer. Cook for 30 minutes, stirring occasionally.

Keep the sauce warm for serving.

<u>To assemble:</u> Preheat the oven to broil.

Split each of the submarine rolls lengthwise, taking care not to cut all the way through. Place 6 meatballs in each roll. Spoon a generous layer of sauce over top, then sprinkle liberally with Parmesan, followed by an ample coating of mozzarella.

Line a baking sheet with foil, place the subs on top, then slide under the broiler for about 5 minutes. Remove from the oven as soon as the cheese is melted and slightly browned.

Serve immediately.

---

*"Health food may be good for the conscience but Oreos taste a hell of a lot better."*
*Robert Redford*

---

# TOTS WITH THE LOT
## Serves 8

---

*INGREDIENTS*
<u>Cheese Sauce</u>
2 tablespoons butter
1 tablespoon shallot, finely chopped
1 tablespoon flour
1/3 cup white wine
1/3 cup milk
2 egg yolks
1 lb. cheddar cheese, extra sharp, grated
Tabasco, to taste

<u>Tots*</u>
1 1/2 lb. potatoes, grated, towel dried
1 cup onion, coarsely grated, drained of excess moisture
1 egg, beaten
1/2 cup breadcrumbs
1 teaspoon baking powder
1 teaspoon salt
1/2 teaspoon black pepper
vegetable oil, for frying

<u>Garnish</u>
1/4 cup Italian parsley, chopped
1/4 cup pickled jalapenos, finely sliced
1/4 cup bacon, cooked, crumbled
1/2 cup Parmesan, grated

*DIRECTIONS*
<u>To make the cheese sauce</u>: Melt the butter in large saucepan over medium high heat. Add the shallot and cook for 5 minutes

until soft, then whisk in the flour. Reduce the heat to medium, then whisk in the wine, a little at a time, maintaining a smooth consistency.

In a separate bowl, whisk together the milk and egg. Slowly whisk this mixture into the sauce. When fully incorporated, add the cheese, a little at a time, whisking to ensure a smooth and creamy sauce. Add a few dashes of Tabasco, to taste. When done, reduce the heat to low, keeping the sauce covered and warm until ready to serve.

To make the tots: In a large bowl, combine the potatoes, onion, egg, breadcrumbs, baking powder, salt and pepper and mix thoroughly.

Pour a 1/4-inch layer of oil into a straight walled sauté pan and place over high heat. When the oil is hot, cooking in small batches, spoon in heaping teaspoons of the potato mixture to make coin sized pancakes (approximately 1 1/2 inches in diameter). Cook until nicely browned, then flip and cook the other side. When fully browned, transfer to a paper towel and allow to drain. Keep the pancakes warm in a 200°F oven until ready to serve.

To serve: Place an equal number of pancakes onto 8 plates. Spoon cheese sauce over each, then garnish with a sprinkle of parsley, jalapeno, bacon and Parmesan. Serve while hot.

*Rather than making your own tots, you can simply buy, heat, and serve ready-made tater tots available in the freezer case from most supermarkets.

 I found myself staring at a mountain of barbecued ribs resting on a foundation of French fries, all topped with kajmak.

In my professional world, I had become a frequent speaker at trade events, typically offering ideas about the benefits associated with well designed brands. Having presented a session at the just concluded Summer Fancy Food Show in New York, I received a surprising phone call asking if I would like to work in Serbia. There were two thoughts that immediately shot through my mind - the first being "Hell yes! That'll be an adventure" and the second being "Where the fuck is Serbia?"

Of course, I said yes, eliminating the expletives and any notion of being completely clueless. The upshot is that I would make repeated visits to Serbia, each lasting anywhere from three to five weeks over a period of about eight years. I would consult with farmers, food processors, and brand owners on topics related to product development, packaging design, marketing best-practices, and export development.

Along the way, I would encounter Serbian and Eastern European foods of every imaginable configuration featuring ingredients, preparation methodologies, and flavor profiles that would consistently surprise and delight my senses. Whether these foods were prepared in restaurants, take-out shops, or in private kitchens, every meal, tasting, and sampling was a highly anticipated and eye-opening occasion.

No matter how long my visit, the hospitality I received was remarkable - far more inviting and gracious than any business encounters at home. This is just one of the many reasons there is a special place in my heart for the people of Serbia.

Even the smallest gestures, typically sweet baked goods that would accompany a cup of coffee or tea, would be warmly offered. Of course, not having experienced foods of any sort from this part of the world, the cookies that accompanied the coffee were frequently exotic, exciting, and provoked animated conversation.

At times, my enthusiasm led to even more food being served or an insistence that we stay longer to enjoy lunch or late afternoon meal together. It was truly amazing how open, inviting, and friendly these people could be.

I also learned that it is considered proper etiquette to share a small glass of brandy, wine, or other such spirits with visitors and esteemed guests. In many cases, the wine or brandy was home made, making it impossible to say no. In addition, drinking these libations provided yet another opportunity to extol the virtues of Serbian food. (Note: I learned that alcoholic beverages could easily be consumed any time of day, even when small glasses of brandy were offered during early morning meetings. Quite simply, it was fun.)

One of the dishes that my colleagues insisted could not be missed was barbeque. Although I initially thought they were referring to something akin to sloppy joe, the term barbeque was used synonymously for grilled meats. Whether it was ribs, steaks, or pljeskavica (a patty made from a blend of ground beef, pork and lamb), there was a discernible sense of pride associated with these dishes.

While I never enjoyed barbeque from Serbia's southernmost city of Lescovac, considered the place for the best barbecue in the country (the best barbecue in the world according to their travel literature), the most noteworthy barbeque I had was served at an unassuming little restaurant just across the street from a colleague's office in nearby Kruševac.

The place was a kafana, more of a pub than a restaurant, set back from the road and nearly invisible to passing traffic, making it a well kept local secret. Unremarkable on the surface, this place was about to rock my world.

Finding myself unable to decipher menus written in Serbian language, many of the meals we enjoyed were organized by trusted companions. It was always a welcome surprise when the food was served. On this particular occasion, when the waiter returned with our order, I found myself staring at a mountain of barbecued ribs resting on a foundation of French fries, all topped with a generous serving of kajmak (a local cheese similar to clotted cream). Unlike anything I had ever seen or tasted before, this dinner would quickly become one of the most remarkable meals I would have in Serbia, and one of the best meals I would ever have... period!

As long as I'm on the subject of grilled meats, another tasty dish is muckalica, a hearty stew made with thin strips of grilled meat (typically pork or beef) along with tomatoes, peppers, and chili. It quickly became one of my favorite and eagerly sought after dishes, one that I would endeavor to have as often as possible.

I also spent a fair amount of time exploring Belgrade's endless variety of street foods, all prepared by vendors who would dispense their creations either from push carts, through little windows in the sides of buildings, or over counters in tiny fast-casual cafes. Whether it was freshly baked pizza, pljeskavica made to order, ćevapčići (ground meat shaped into small sausages) hot off the grill, or palacinke (crepes) served sweet with Plazma cookie crumbs and preserves or savory with ham and cheese fillings, every one of these hand-held snacks was just as satisfying as the multi-course meals I'd have in fancier sit-down restaurants.

I have to admit that, out of all of the street foods available, palacinke was my favorite - especially the ones filled with mushrooms, sour cream and cheese. As I wandered the city, I would make note of the shops that maintained palacinke cooktops, making these places easier to find later on. Whether it was time for lunch, a casual snack, or late night indulgence, these would be the places I'd seek out on a regular basis.

Of course, it would be irresponsible of me to overlook the endless variety of sweet treats available throughout the city, especially along Knez Mihailova, the cafe-lined pedestrian thoroughfare in the center of town. With its never ending stream of glamorous and well-heeled fashionistas, it was easy to spend hours sipping coffee, nibbling on sensationally sweet cakes, or spooning creamy mounds of incredibly rich gelato while watching the passing parade.

Although Knez Mihailova offered an abundance of pleasurable distractions, my all time favorite destination for desserts was Mamma's Biscuit House, a charming little cafe in one of the oldest surviving residential neighborhoods in the city. Renown for their cakes, tarts, and cookies, I was drawn to their bite-sized confections, artfully designed to look like miniature sheep, pigs, bumble bees, and cows. Whenever time would permit, I'd race over for a quick cup of coffee and munch on a few of these exquisite little critters. When invited to dinner parties, these little guys were always a welcomed treat.

It's important to mention that Serbia has an enormous agricultural community that distributes fresh and delicious fruits, vegetables, grains, dairy products, and meats to restaurants and outdoor markets around the country on a regular basis. Needless to say, attending an open-air farmer's market on the weekends is an eye-opening and mouth-watering affair.

Three items in particular stand out - the tremendous variety of farm-made white cheeses, the omnipresence of cabbage, and the abundance of locally-grown peppers (capsicum). When it comes to traditional Serbian meals, these foods are mainstays in both home-cooked and professionally prepared meals.

White cheese, served alongside freshly baked bread, was standard fare and always eagerly anticipated. Equally common were fresh vegetables including cabbage, tomato, cucumber, and pepper, served freshly sliced, marinated or grilled.

Once the cheese and vegetables were served, they would be followed by a shopska salad - a traditional Balkan dish overflowing with sliced tomatoes and cucumbers, all topped with a thick blanket of grated white cheese, a sprinkle of oil and a splash of vinegar.

I soon realized that cabbage would inevitably find its way onto the table during just about every meal. Whether it was offered as a stand alone vegetable or incorporated into a more complex recipe, it is an unmistakable mainstay in local cuisine. While I enjoyed numerous variations of marinated and cooked cabbage, the dish that delighted me the most was sarma - cabbage leaves wrapped firmly around a mixture of rice and meat, then baked in a rich tomato sauce. Although there are countless variations served throughout Russia and Eastern Europe, I prefer the Serbian recipe.

While cabbage was ubiquitous, peppers (capsicum) were equally popular in Serbian cuisine. Other than fresh configurations, one of the more distinctive dishes is ajvar (pronounced EYE-var). More of a spread than a side dish, it is a fabulously delicious condiment that features roasted red peppers blended with a touch of sunflower oil and garlic. While numerous variations can be found that incorporate ingredients such as tomatoes, hot peppers and eggplant, I prefer ajvar that's made simply with roasted red peppers.

It's important to note that Serbia has a population of more than 7 million individuals with diverse ethnic backgrounds. As such, there are foods served in one part of the country that are unheard of in others - a dynamic I experienced while working in the southwestern city of Novi Pazar.

The dish that captivated my attention was mantije (pronounced MAHN-tee-yay). These were small, pastry-wrapped parcels of ground meat akin to baked Chinese dim sum. When you factor in my love for all things dumpling-like, it's not surprising that I became obsessed with mantije.

As mentioned, mantije were not found, or even recognized,

in other parts of Serbia. The good news is that I found a somewhat different presentation served in a restaurant in Belgrade. Rather than presented plain, this surprisingly delicious version had the mantije smothered in a rich white garlic sauce and baked until the dish was bubbly hot and nicely browned.

While I have yet to find a recipe that yields a finished product anything like those in Novi Pazar, or even the dish prepared in Belgrade, it is a quest that I will eventually complete.

Serbia's proximity to Italy, a short jump by air and a relatively easy drive by road, is another factor that has influenced Serbian cuisine. It's not surprising that some of the best Italian foods I have ever encountered (also to the south in Montenegro - see the next chapter) was in Serbia.

Considering the plethora of Italian restaurants, securing a comforting dish of pasta and a relaxing glass of wine was easy. There were, however, a few instances where I would be served pasta in a meaty ragu (sauce) infinitely better than anything I had tasted before. Needless to say, I would inhale these dishes with so much glee, relish, and gusto that my dining companions would end up giving me these sidelong, somewhat concerned, looks of disbelief. Whether the ragu was served with tortellini, linguini, fettuccini, or pappardelle, there would never be a serving large enough to satisfy my appetite.

# SERBIAN AJVAR
Makes 2 cups

---

*INGREDIENTS*
8 red capsicums
2 tablespoons tomato paste
2 teaspoons sunflower oil
1 teaspoon salt

*DIRECTIONS*
Roast the peppers over a gas flame or under a broiler until skin is charred on all sides. Transfer to a large bowl and cover completely, allowing peppers to rest for 20 minutes. When cool enough to handle, carefully peel and seed the capsicums (NOTE: Do not clean roasted capsicum under running water as this will wash away much of the roasted flavor). Place the cleaned capsicum flesh in a large colander and allow to drain thoroughly - at least 2 hours.

Transfer drained capsicum to a food processor. Pulse in small intervals to achieve a consistently chunky texture (ajvar is meant to be chunky, not smooth). Transfer to a clean mixing bowl, then fold in the tomato paste, oil and salt.

If you like things spicy, try adding a few dashes of hot sauce. Hellacious!

Keep refrigerated. Serve at room temperature.

Serving Tip: Make bruschetta with 1/2 inch slices of crusty baguette, spread with a little ajvar, sprinkle with a little fresh basil, parsley and/or cilantro, top with a nice white cheese (ricotta, Parmesan or mozzarella). Place under the broiler until bubbly hot, then serve.

# MUĆKALICA
Serves 8

---

*INGREDIENTS*
3 tablespoons peanut oil
2 lb. pork loin, thinly sliced, cut into 1/2-inch strips
2 tablespoons butter
3 onions, thinly sliced
1 teaspoon garlic, minced
1 green bell pepper, cut into strips
1 red bell pepper, cut into strips
1 cup beef stock
1 1/2 teaspoon Kosher salt
2 teaspoons sweet paprika
1/2 teaspoon cayenne
1/4 cup tomato paste
1 lb. wide egg noodles, cooked
4 oz. feta cheese, crumbled

*DIRECTIONS*
Pour the oil into a large Dutch oven over medium high heat. Add the pork and cook until brown, about 10 minutes. Using a slotted spoon, transfer the pork into a bowl and set aside.

In the same pot, add the butter, onions and garlic and cook until soft. Add the green and red peppers and cook for 5 minutes. Add the pork followed by the stock, salt, paprika, cayenne and pepper. Bring to a boil, then reduce to simmer. Cover and cook for 1 hour, stirring every 15 minutes or so to prevent sticking. Add the tomato paste and continue cooking for another 30 minutes.

Serve over wide egg noodles with a sprinkle of crumbled feta.

# MUSHROOM & SWISS PALACINKE
Makes 6 - 8 palacinke

_____

## INGREDIENTS
1 tablespoon olive oil
16 oz. mushrooms, thinly sliced, fully cooked and drained
1/4 cup sour cream
2 large eggs, beaten
1 cup flour
3/4 cup milk
1/2 cup water
3 tablespoons butter, melted; plus additional butter for coating the pan
1/2 lb. Swiss cheese, grated

## DIRECTIONS
Place the olive oil in a sauté pan over medium high heat. Add the mushrooms and cook until all of the water has evaporated.

Transfer the mushrooms to a bowl, add the sour cream, mix thoroughly and set aside.

To make the pancake batter, whisk together the eggs, flour, milk, water, and butter in a large bowl.

Place a large flat griddle or frying pan over high heat. Rub the pan with butter, making sure to coat the entire surface.

Reduce the heat to medium high, then ladle enough batter to make a thin 12" pancake. Use a spatula to spread out the batter or simply tilt the pan in all directions.

As the pancake cooks, it will become dry enough to lift. This is when you spread a little of the mushroom mixture, followed by a sprinkle of cheese, on half of the pancake. Once the cheese has started to melt, fold the pancake in half so that the mushrooms and cheese are completely covered. Continue cooking for another minute or until the pancake begins to brown. Transfer the crepe to a platter, fold in thirds to create a triangle, and serve.

NOTE: When purchased from street vendors, the folded crepe is wrapped in a paper sleeve and eaten with hands.

---

*"There's no better feeling in the world than a warm pizza box on your lap."*
*Kevin James*

---

# PAPPARDELLE WITH MEATY RAGU
## Serves 8

---

*INGREDIENTS*
1/4 cup olive oil
2 cups onion, finely chopped
1 cup carrot, finely chopped
1 cup red capsicum, finely chopped
3 tablespoons garlic, minced, divided
3 lb. beef, trimmed, cut into 1/2" cubes
3 lb. pork, trimmed, cut into 1/2 " cubes
2 cups beef stock
2 cups red wine, divided
2 cups tomato purée
2 teaspoons crushed red pepper
1 teaspoon salt
1/2 cup fresh basil chiffonade, plus more for garnish
3 lb. dry pappardelle
2 cups grated Parmesan, plus more for the table

*DIRECTIONS*
Pour the olive oil into a large stock pot over medium high heat. Add the onions, carrots, red capsicum, 1 tablespoon minced garlic and sauté until the vegetables are soft.

Add the beef and pork, a little at a time, allowing the meats to brown. Once all of the meat has browned, add the stock, 1 cup of the wine, and bring to a boil. Reduce the heat to a simmer and let cook, stirring occasionally, for 1 1/2 hours.

Add the remaining wine and all of the puree and continue cooking for another 1 1/2 hours.

Add the remaining garlic, crushed red pepper, salt and cook

for one more hour. Add water, if needed, to keep the sauce loose and avoid burning. Continue cooking until the meats have broken down and a nice thick sauce is formed.

Add the basil and check for flavor, adding more salt, as needed.

Cook the pappardelle according to directions, then drain.

To serve, distribute the pappardelle equally on all of the plates, spoon some of the ragu over top, sprinkle generously with grated Parmesan and garnish with basil. Be sure to have extra grated Parmesan on the table for those who want more.

---

*"A balanced diet is a cookie in each hand."*
*Barbara Johnson*

---

# SARMA - STUFFED CABBAGE
Makes 12 pieces

---

*INGREDIENTS*
1 large cabbage

Filling
3/4 lb. ground pork
3/4 lb. ground beef
1/2 cup white rice, uncooked
1 cup onion, finely chopped
2 eggs, beaten
1/2 cup water
1 tablespoon garlic, minced
1 1/2 teaspoons salt
1/2 teaspoon pepper

Sauce
2 tablespoons olive oil
1 cup onion, finely chopped
1/4 cup raisins, finely chopped
1/4 cup brown sugar, lightly packed
3 cups crushed tomatoes (canned)
2 tablespoons red wine vinegar
1 teaspoon salt
1/2 teaspoon black pepper

*DIRECTIONS*
Fill a very large stockpot three-quarters full with water and
bring to a rapid boil.

Using a paring knife, cut and remove the core of the cabbage.
Insert a large fork into the cavity, then carefully immerse the
whole cabbage into the boiling water. As the cabbage softens,

the outer leaves will begin to fall away. Allow them to cook for about a minute, then transfer to a large tray to drain and cool. Repeat this process with the entire head, until all of the cabbage leaves have been removed

Once cooled, shave off a layer of the thick center spine on each leaf so that it will be thinner and easier to roll. When completed, set the 12 largest leaves aside for rolling. The remaining leaves will be used for cooking or reserved for another use.

To make the filling: Combine the pork, beef, rice, onion, eggs, water, garlic, salt and pepper, cover and refrigerate for 1 hour.

To make the sauce: Place a large saucepan over medium high heat. Pour in the olive oil, then stir in the onions and cook for about 2 minutes. Add the raisins and continue cooking for another 5 minutes. Stir in the brown sugar, followed by the tomatoes, vinegar, salt and pepper. Bring to a boil, then reduce to a simmer and cook for 30 minutes. When done, remove from the heat and set aside.

To make the cabbage rolls, place a large cabbage leaf on a flat surface with the spine running vertically. Spoon approximately 1/3 cup of the filling onto the leaf, then roll it up tightly, folding in the sides as you roll. Repeat this process until all of the filling has been used.

Cover the bottom of a Dutch oven with a layer of the remaining cabbage leaves. Cover the leaves with half the sauce, then fit the rolled cabbage in tight rows on top. If a second layer is needed, spoon a small amount of sauce over top, then arrange the second layer. Spoon all of the remaining sauce over top, then cover and bake in a 400F degrees oven for 1 1/2 hours.

# SHOPSKA SALAD
## Serves 4

---

*INGREDIENTS*
4 oz. baby spinach leaves, washed and patted dry
2 cups grape tomatoes, halved
2 cups cucumber, peeled, seeded, halved and sliced
1/4 cup red onion, diced
8 oz. white cheese,* grated
1/4 cup olive oil
3 tablespoons balsamic vinegar
1 teaspoon orange zest
1/2 teaspoon black pepper
salt, to taste

*DIRECTIONS*
Distribute the spinach leaves equally onto four salad plates, followed by single layers of the tomatoes, cucumber, onion, and white cheese (there should be an abundance of cheese covering the salad on each plate).

In a separate bowl, whisk together the oil, vinegar, zest, and pepper to make a vinaigrette. Add salt as needed. Just before serving, drizzle a little of the vinaigrette over top of each salad.

*In Serbia, there are as many white cheeses as there are cheese makers. Adding to the confusion, most countries throughout the Balkans, and even around the world, have their own versions of white cheese. For authenticity, see what you can find at ethnic stores that cater to Eastern Europeans. Alternatively, Monterey Jack, Mozzarella or Mexican Fresco (crumbling cheese), all relatively easy to come by, will suffice.

 At the end of the meal, the owner would offer a small glass of his house made limoncello. While Australia taught me "sticky," Montenegro would teach me limoncello.

**A**lthough not yet accustomed to working overseas (I had only just completed my first assignment in Serbia), I knew that another job would provide sure-fire relief from the heartbreak of my impending divorce. As such, I eagerly accepted an assignment in Montenegro. For at least a few weeks, the dramas at home would be out of sight and out of mind. In addition, I was sure there would be new and exciting gastronomic encounters that would lighten my mood.

It's important to note that Podgorica, the capital city of Montenegro, was considerably smaller and less developed than Belgrade. As such, the number of worthwhile restaurants and street vendors were few, creating limited opportunities to encounter foods of note.

Having befriended an American expat living and working full time in Podgorica, we ended up spending a significant amount of time after work and on weekends comparing notes about our experiences in town, happily sipping away on gin & tonics for hours on end, and watching the pedestrian parade that passed by the outdoor cafés we frequented. Judging by the remarkable fashions that caught our eyes, it was apparent that locals (at least among the younger, cool and groovy set) invested heavily in their wardrobe.

As with Serbia, Montenegro's proximity to Italy meant that I would have easy access to remarkable Italian food. Since one of my clients was a locally-based cheesemaker specializing in Italian-style cheeses, I had access to the most extraordinary mozzarella I've ever tasted. I even got a tour of the cheese making facility, watching the mozzarella being pulled and stretched, then shaped into small balls or braided into twists. It's fascinating to watch.

The other foods of Italian origin that impressed me the most came from one of the local restaurants. While I cannot recall its name, frequent visits allowed me to enjoy their tortellini Bolognese on multiple, very happy, occasions. Rich, slightly sweet, and meaty, I could never get enough. It was interesting to note that the Bolognese was never quite the same from day to day. Sometimes it leaned towards tomato and beefiness, other times a bit richer and creamier. Regardless, creating a Bolognese as good as theirs has been an ongoing challenge that I have yet to resolve. Other than the fresh mozzarella previously mentioned, this was the most astounding flavor sensation I would experience in Montenegro.

It's important to note that, when you make so many repeated visits, there's a level of familiarity and camaraderie that gets established with restaurateurs. I was always greeted warmly upon arrival, service was impeccable, and meals were consistently delicious. Although I never stopped obsessing over their Bolognese, one of the most delightful moments came at the end of the meal when the owner would offer a small glass of his house-made limoncello. While Australia had taught me to finish a meal with a glass of "sticky," Montenegro would teach me to wind things up with limoncello.

I have since learned that limoncello is not that difficult to make. It does, however, take care, patience, and about a month to become a truly flavorful treat.

It goes without saying that travel frequently imposes situations that are, to say the least, a bit quirky. At the time of my visit, ordering wine was a limited proposition. No matter where I dined, the choices were always Chardonnay, Cabernet, Merlot or Vranac Pro Corde. There were no wine lists, no brands to choose from, just these four standard options.

With newfound friendships, I was also introduced to Podgorica's vibrant night life, learning how much fun could be had when working overseas in strange and unusual places. At one point well into the wee hours of the morning, we were part of a jubilant crowd packed into a night club, dancing and singing along with the band. I have no idea what we were singing but it was fun. Really fun.

# FETTUCCINE AL RAGU
### Serves 6

---

*INGREDIENTS*
1/4 cup olive oil
1/2 cup carrot, finely chopped
1/2 cup onion, finely chopped
1 red capsicum, finely chopped
1/2 lb. pancetta, finely diced
1 1/2 lb. beef (for stew), cut into 1/2-inch cubes
3/4 cup dry red wine
28 oz. (can) crushed tomatoes
1 tablespoon chicken bouillon
2 bay leaves
1 tablespoon crushed red pepper
1/2 teaspoon sugar
1/2 teaspoon salt
1/2 teaspoon pepper
1 lb. dry fettuccine
Parmesan cheese, grated
1/2 cup ricotta

*DIRECTIONS*
Heat the oil in a large Dutch oven. Add the carrot, onion and capsicum and sauté until soft. Add the pancetta and continue cooking for 5 minutes. Add the beef and cook until all liquid has evaporated. Add the wine and cook once again, until all liquid has evaporated. Add the tomatoes, bouillon, bay leaves and pepper, bring to a boil, then reduce to a simmer.

Cook for 90 minutes, stirring occasionally, until the beef is tender and breaks apart easily. Add the sugar, salt, and pepper, adjusting as needed, to taste.

When the sauce is ready to serve, prepare the fettuccine according to directions.

Distribute the cooked fettuccine evenly into 6 bowls. Top with sauce, followed by a generous portion of grated Parmesan and a dollop of ricotta.

---

*"People who love to eat
are always the best people."*
*Julia Child*

---

# FRESH RICOTTA
Makes approximately 2 cups

---

*INGREDIENTS*
7 cups whole milk (not ultra pasteurized)
1 cup heavy cream
3 teaspoons kosher salt
5 tablespoons distilled white vinegar

*DIRECTIONS*
Place the milk and cream in a Dutch oven over medium high heat. Bring the temperature of the liquid to 200°F, stirring occasionally to avoid burning. Once this temperature is reached, remove from heat, stir in the vinegar and salt, then let rest for appx 10 minutes.

Place several layers of cheesecloth (if large enough, simply fold to fit) over a colander, then pour in the cheese mixture. Allow the curds to drain for about 1 hour, then discard the liquid.

The finished ricotta can be stored in a covered, air tight container for about 3 days.

# LIMONCELLO
Makes 2 liters

---

*INGREDIENTS*
13 lemons
1 L grain alcohol
1 L water
1 kg sugar

*DIRECTIONS*
Carefully remove the yellow portion of the rind on all of the lemons, avoiding the white pith.

Place the rinds and grain alcohol in a large bottle or storage jar that can be tightly sealed (making sure it is large enough to hold all of the ingredients). Shake this mixture, once a day, for 20 days.

After 20 days, make the sugar solution. Place the water in a large pot and bring to a boil. Remove from heat, add the sugar, and stir until it is fully dissolved. Allow the sugar solution to cool completely.

Once the sugar solution is fully cooled, add it to the alcohol, mix together and reseal the container. Continue shaking this liquid, once a day, for an additional 10 days. After 10 days, your Limoncello is ready.

Limoncello is best served chilled.

# TOMATO BASIL AND CHEESE SALAD
### Serves 4

---

*INGREDIENTS*
Vinaigrette
1/3 cup olive oil
3 tablespoon balsamic vinegar
1 tablespoon Dijon mustard
1/2 teaspoon garlic, finely minced
salt and pepper to taste

Salad
1 red tomato, cut into 8 thin slices
1 yellow tomato, cut into 8 thin slices
1 large ball fresh mozzarella, cut into 12 thin slices
1 bunch fresh green basil
1 bunch fresh purple basil, if available
1/2 cup fresh ricotta
1 or 2 oranges, supremed (you will need 12 supremes)*
sliced or crushed almonds, for garnish (optional)

*DIRECTIONS*
To make the vinaigrette: Whisk all of the ingredients together.
Add salt and pepper as needed, to taste. This dressing should
be made a few hours in advance.

To make the salad: Arrange 4 slices tomato, 3 slices mozzarella,
and 6 basil leaves on each plate, alternating one ingredient
after the next to create a rainbow effect. Place a dollop of
ricotta and three orange supremes on top.

Drizzle a little vinaigrette, sprinkle with almonds, and serve.

*There are videos online that show how to supreme citrus.

 There wasn't much of a local food industry. The majority of products on supermarket shelves were imported, bearing names including Oreo, Cap'n Crunch, Nestlé, and Oscar Meyer.

**W**hen I was asked to develop a public relations program for the Ministry of Finance in Guyana, I thought I was going to Ghana. Good thing Google Earth had been invented and I double checked. When I realized I would be going to South America instead of Africa, I got excited, believing this would be an opportunity for me to practice my Spanish language skills. Once I started poking around online to learn more about the place prior to arrival, I discovered that English was their native tongue. So, I didn't go to Africa and I didn't speak Spanish. C'est la vie.

I also learned that I would be staying in the capital city of Georgetown, known to be a bit rough around the edges and not entirely safe for visitors. Even the staff at the hotel warned me about the potential for muggings and admonished me not to wander about. Knowing that satisfying my curiosity was not as important as securing my well being, I put myself under hotel arrest, venturing out only when a staff car was available to take me to the office or shopping for essentials.

Since potentially dangerous conditions, even going out for dinner, prevented me from eating my way through town, and my work did not require me to engage with local food producers, the variety and quality of foods I experienced was quite limited. My meals consisted primarily of whatever the hotel restaurant had to offer or the few snacks I would purchase at the nearby supermarket.

After my first visit to the supermarket, it was apparent that there wasn't much of a local food industry in Guyana. In fact, the majority of products on its shelves were imported, bearing brand names including Oreo, Cap'n Crunch, Nestlé, Kraft, Butterball, and Oscar Meyer. With so many highly recognizable American products, I felt like I was shopping at home. While I certainly could have seen and purchased a significantly greater variety of indigenous foods at the Stabroek Market, a large open market operating in the city center, this was considered one of the riskier places to stroll about, especially for distracted tourists.

Ultimately, my culinary experiences would be limited to the foods served at the hotel. With a buffet that changed daily, I was exposed to numerous local dishes including curries, cook-up rice (a casserole of rice, beans, and meat), pepperpot (a rich beef stew made with cassareep and cinnamon) and a non-alcoholic beverage called mauby (made from the bark of a mauby tree, cinnamon, and sugar). Sadly, the buffet left a lot to be desired so my enthusiasm at mealtimes was somewhat diminished.

The saving grace, and truly the only reason I felt compelled to include Guyana in this book, was the time I spent at the hotel bar. Before I arrived in Georgetown, my cocktail of choice was either a vodka martini or scotch on the rocks. Upon arrival, however, I noticed a plethora of promotional posters, ads, and other branded touchpoints exclaiming the virtues of locally produced El Dorado rum. At the bar itself, I spied a row of bottles, all prominently displayed and bearing El Dorado labels.

Having a well developed practice of sampling indigenous foods and drinks, I asked the bartender about this domestic spirit. What I learned, and more importantly, what I tasted, would change my drinking habits for the rest of my life.

For the uninitiated, rum in Guyana (and throughout the Caribbean) had been made by a variety of distillers since the early 1800's. By 1998, many had merged or been amalgamated to form a single entity - Demerara Distillers Limited.

Operating from a facility on the eastern banks of the Demerara River, the company now enjoys worldwide distribution and a reputation for rums of distinction. It's mainstream line, comprised of 12-year, 15-year and 21-year cask aged rums, delivers a wonderful sweetness indicative of sugar cane (the spirit's base ingredient) along with more distinctive and sophisticated flavor notes.

Knowing that I would not be venturing out into the city during my free time, and especially on weekends, I would mosey up to the bar. Starting with the youngest bottle, then working my way up to the oldest, I would sample one rum after another. With time on my side, it was always fun to go backwards, starting with the 21-year bottle, drinking my way into the younger 15-year bottle and subsequently the 12-year bottle.

Over a period of two weeks, this would be my routine. Up the line, then back down. It was fun and delicious.

Once home, I was eager to learn more about Caribbean rums, especially those displaying more robust flavor profiles. While my explorations are far from comprehensive, and El Dorado remains an all time favorite, I have since discovered Pyrat, Ron Zacapa, Plantation, Flor de Cana, Bumbu, Papa's Pilar, Kirk and Sweeney, The Real McCoy, and Diplomatico to name just a few. Depending on my mood, they are all my favorites.

While I'm not sure if it's safer to visit Georgetown these days, I highly recommend adding a bottle of El Dorado rum to your home bar. You'll also want to invite a few friends over for a drink or three, then sit back, relax, and embark on your own tropical adventure.

# PEPPERPOT
## Serves 8

---

*INGREDIENTS*
4 tablespoons peanut oil
4 lb. beef (for stew), cut into 1-inch cubes
1 cup onion, diced
1 tablespoon garlic, minced
2 Scotch Bonnet or Habanero chilies, finely chopped
1 cup cassareep*
3 sticks cinnamon
1 orange, zested
1/2 cup brown sugar
1 teaspoon Kosher salt
2 teaspoons thyme
3 cups water

*DIRECTIONS*
Pour the vegetable oil into a large Dutch oven over medium high heat. Add the beef, cooking until fully browned.

Add the onion, garlic, and chilies and cook for an additional 10 minutes.

Add the cassareep, cinnamon sticks, orange zest, brown sugar, salt, thyme, water, and stir. Bring the stew to a boil, then reduce the heat to low. Cover and cook for 2 hours, stirring occasionally. At the end of 2 hours, cook uncovered, for 1 more hour. Add water if needed.

Serve with rice or thick slices of bread to soak up the sauce.

*Cassareep is a thick, molasses-like substance available in ethnic grocery stores specializing in Caribbean foods.

# CLASSIC RUM COCKTAILS
Each recipe makes 1 cocktail

---

## RUM PUNCH
Makes 1 cocktail

*INGREDIENTS*
1 1/2 ounces dark rum
1/4 ounce grenadine
2 ounces pineapple juice
club soda, as needed
1 pineapple slice, for garnish

*DIRECTIONS*
Place a handful of ice cubes in a cocktail shaker. Add the rum, grenadine and juice, cover and shake. Strain into an 8-ounce cocktail glass filled with ice, then top with club soda. Garnish with a slice of pineapple and serve.

## CLASSIC DAIQUIRI
Makes 1 cocktail

*INGREDIENTS*
1 1/2 ounces rum
3/4 ounce lime juice (fresh)
1/4 ounce simple syrup*

*DIRECTIONS*
Place a handful of ice cubes in a cocktail shaker. Add the rum, lime juice, and simple syrup, cover and shake. Strain into an 8-ounce cocktail glass filled with ice and serve.

*Simple Syrup
Combine 1 cup hot water with 1 cup granulated sugar. Stir until fully dissolved. Chill until needed.

## HURRICANE
Makes 1 1/2 quarts

*INGREDIENTS*
1 3/4 cups light rum
1 1/4 cups dark rum
1 1/2 cups fresh orange juice
1 1/2 cups pineapple juice
1/2 cup cranberry juice
1/2 cup sour mix*
2 tablespoons grenadine
orange slices, for garnish
maraschino cherries, for garnish

*DIRECTIONS*
Combine ingredients in a large pitcher and mix well. Serve over ice. Garnish with orange slices and maraschino cherries.

*Sour Mix
12 ounce lemon juice (appx 6 lemons)
18 ounce water
1/4 cup sugar
1 egg white
Keeps no more than 7 - 10 days

 **RUSSIA** I looked forward to sampling Russian vodka. For me, Russia and vodka has the same relationship as Italy and pasta, Paris and crepes, or New York and hot dogs.

I grew up during a time when the Soviet Union was considered America's fiercest enemy. It was assumed that Russians were out to destroy us and could not be trusted. Jumping forward a few decades, I found myself heading to Moscow under significantly different circumstances to work with and support Russian food producers. I would have the opportunity to get a glimpse of the Russian landscape, sample their foods, and completely debunk any lingering negativity about the country and its people.

My work did not take place in the big cities. In fact, other than a one-day briefing upon arrival in Moscow, my time would be spent several hundred miles to the south in the region known as Stavropol krai, not far from the Caucasus mountains and Russia's southern border shared with Georgia.

For the record, my clients were incredibly warm, friendly, and hospitable. Although we did not speak each other's language (I relied on a translator to assist with communication the entire time), we worked well together, ate well together, and enjoyed each other's company immensely. In fact, I had never been made to feel so at home, so quickly, anywhere else prior to this visit.

When it came to food, other than eggs and toast for breakfast, the majority of my meals were eye-openers, the most note-worthy being their mayonnaise based salads. Whether it was potato salad, tuna salad, egg salad, or chicken salad, all of the ingredients were cut into tiny dice-sized cubes, then drowned in mayonnaise. In addition, these dishes tended to have all sorts of added vegetables, herbs and spices that changed their flavor and intensified their foreign-ness. None were off-putting, just dramatically different from what I ex-pected. Considering how frequently they were served, it took a little getting used to.

I must admit, the one thing I looked forward to the most was Russian-made vodka. For me, Russia and vodka have the same relationship as Italy and pasta, Paris and crepes, or New York and hot dogs. For those who remember the song "Love and Marriage" made popular by Frank Sinatra in the mid-1950s, you could change the lyrics to include "Russia and vodka" (although the cadence and rhyme would be way off kilter).

In Russia, vodka was generally served in small carafes accom-panied by enough shot glasses for everyone at the table, similar to the way sake is served in Japanese restaurants. I would also learn that, if you're going to drink vodka, it is appropriate to include a plate of smoked salmon, pickled cornichons, chopped red onion, and capers. Blinis with caviar and sour cream were also excellent companions, although somewhat more expensive.

The other thing about drinking vodka is that, in the company of Russians, each shot is preceded by a toast - a praiseworthy comment about the guests at the table, their remarkable accomplishments, or their country of origin. This was certainly the case at all of the dinners I attended. We toasted each other constantly, and I would wake up the following morning with a hangover as proof.

Since the majority of us grew up during the cold war era, we would recall times when Russians feared Americans as much as Americans feared Russians. Recognizing our shared history, a common toast would comment upon how much we enjoyed each other's company, something that years before would have been impossible to imagine.

Considering the Russian love and popularity of smoked and pickled fish, it was not surprising to find herring-based dishes showing up on menus. Since I have always enjoyed its distinctive flavor, I would blindly order herring whenever available.

On one particular occasion, I found it featured in a dish called "Herring Wearing a Fur Coat." Thinking the menu had been humorously translated into English (research indicates this curious moniker is actually its proper name), I was compelled to investigate further.

Consisting of grated potato, beets, carrots, red onion, and chopped herring, this artfully layered salad offers remarkable contrasts in terms of both flavors and colors that makes for an eye-catching and wholly engaging presentation.

While I would have plenty of thoroughly enjoyable meals, no

dish was as appealing as pelmenes. If you have not had the pleasure, they are tiny, meat-filled dumplings akin to tortellini. Filled with either ground pork, lamb or beef, or a mixture of meats, these toothsome morsels are cooked in boiling water, drained, then topped with butter and sour cream. Considering my love of dumplings in general, whether Italian, Chinese, Polish or otherwise, it should be no surprise that I'd order pelmenes whenever possible.

All of these events took place about 150 miles north of Russia's southern border along the Caucasus mountains (shared with the country of Georgia). Not too many years later, I would be engaged to work with a variety of food producers in Georgia as well.

# BORSCHT
## Serves 10

---

*INGREDIENTS*
6 cups vegetable stock
2 cups beets, finely grated
2 cups carrots, finely grated
1 can dark red kidney beans, drained
2 cups red cabbage, thinly sliced
1 onion, thinly sliced
2 cups red potatoes, cut into 1/2-inch cubes
6 oz. tomato paste
2 tablespoons ketchup
5 cloves garlic, minced
1 tablespoon sugar
1 tablespoon lemon juice
1 teaspoon salt
1/2 teaspoon black pepper
For garnish: sour cream, chopped cilantro, and lemon zest

*DIRECTIONS*
Bring the stock to a boil. Add the beets, carrots, beans and cabbage. Bring to a boil, then simmer for 30 minutes.

While the stock is simmering, sauté the onion until soft.

After 30 minutes, add the sautéed onions, potatoes, tomato paste, ketchup, garlic, sugar, and lemon juice. Add salt and pepper, a little at a time, to taste.

Continue to simmer for another 20 minutes, making sure the potatoes are fully cooked.

Serve with a dollop of sour cream and a sprinkle of cilantro.

# HERRING WEARING A FUR COAT
## Serves 4

---

*INGREDIENTS*
1/2 lb. marinated herring (in brine), finely chopped
1lb. white potato, cooked, coarsely grated
1/2 lb. beets, cooked, coarsely grated
1/2 lb. carrots, coarsely grated
1 red onion (small), finely chopped
1/2 cup mayonnaise
assorted greens, for serving

Special Tools
- 3" wide x 2" high pastry ring (or empty vegetable can with top and bottom removed)
- Squirt bottle or pastry bag fitted with a small nozzle

*DIRECTIONS*
This is a layered salad. Make sure you have all of the ingredients prepared in advance of assembly.

Place a small amount of mixed greens on each plate as the foundation for this recipe.

Working one plate at a time, center the pastry ring over the greens. Form a 1/4 inch layer of grated potato followed by a thin layer of herring (not too much - the flavor is strong), a 1/8-inch layer of beets and a 1/8-inch layer of carrots.

Gently lift the pastry ring so that the stacked salad remains vertical and erect.

Drizzle mayonnaise over the top in a decorative manner, followed by a light sprinkling of red onion.

# PELMENI (RUSSIAN DUMPLINGS)
Makes about 90 pelmeni

*INGREDIENTS*

Dough

1/2 cup buttermilk

1 tablespoon sour cream

1 large egg

1 teaspoon salt

3 cups flour

1 cup warm water

Filling

1 tablespoon olive oil

1 onion, finely diced

3 cloves garlic, minced

1 lb. ground pork

1/2 teaspoon salt

1/2 teaspoon ground pepper

Toppings

butter

sour cream

*DIRECTIONS*

To make the dough: Using a food processor, pulse together the buttermilk, sour cream, egg and salt. Slowly add the flour and half the water, alternating between each, until they are fully incorporated. Add the remainder of the water, a little at a time, until a dough has formed.

To make the filling: Heat 1 tbsp oil in a large skillet. Add the onion and sauté until golden and soft. Add the garlic and sauté for another minute, then remove from the heat.

In a large bowl, combine the onion and garlic with the pork, salt, and pepper. Allow to cool.

To assemble the pelmenes: Place a portion of the dough on a lightly floured surface and roll out to make a very thin sheet. Using a 2-inch circle cutter, cut out as many circles as possible.

Place 1 teaspoon of the filling in the center of each circle, fold the dough in half and pinch the edges to seal. Fold the corners over to form a diaper shape and pinch together.

Place the pelmeni onto a well-floured surface, sprinkle with flour, transfer to an air-tight container and freeze. Once frozen, the pelmeni can be placed loosely in a large freezer bag for future use.

To cook the pelmenes: Bring a 4-quart pot of salted water to a boil. Add the frozen pelmeni, cooking until they start to float. Boil for just 3 minutes longer, then drain thoroughly.

Serve with a drizzle of melted butter and a dollop of sour cream.

# RUSSIAN BRUSCHETTA
Serves 8 - 10

---

*INGREDIENTS*
1 cup ricotta
1/4 cup mayonnaise
1 teaspoon garlic, pasted, divided
salt and pepper, to taste
3 tablespoons butter, softened
1 baguette, cut into 1/2 inch slices
1 cup red capsicum, small dice
1 cup tomatoes, small dice
1/4 C basil, chiffonade*

*DIRECTIONS*
In a large mixing bowl, combine the ricotta, 1/2 teaspoon garlic and mayonnaise, then add salt and pepper to taste.

In a small bowl, combine the butter with the remaining garlic.

To assemble, spread a little of the garlic butter onto each slice of bread, then place under a broiler for about 5 minutes until nicely browned. Remove from the oven and allow to cool.

Spread a small amount of the ricotta mixture onto each slice of baguette, followed by a little capsicum and tomato. Sprinkle a few ribbons of basil over top and serve.

* Chiffonade is a technique where you tightly roll a stack of basil leaves (or any large leafed herb), then cut the roll cross-wise into very thin ribbons.

 While Malbec remains one of my favorites, Bonarda became my new best friend. I found its deep ruby color and notes of rich red fruit both alluring and delicious.

**U**nlike longer-term engagements with food growers and processors around the world, I went to Buenos Aires to lead a week-long marketing program that had been organized by the George Washington University's School of Business. We travelled as a group, made our way around town on chartered buses, had a pre-planned agenda that occupied most of our time (including meals), leaving little opportunity for culinary adventures. The good news is that many of the restaurants we dined at as a group offered glimpses into authentic local cuisine. Of course, whenever personal time became available, I made sure to visit the more intimate shops and cafes around the city that shunned tourist-filled buses.

In spite of our group's size, we were adequately exposed to Argentinian culture and many of the delights that Buenos Aires has to offer. In particular, our visit to San Telmo - the oldest neighborhood in Buenos Aires - introduced us to the brightly colored, ornamental, and somewhat fanciful wall graphics and signage that embraced a design style unique to the region known as "Fileteado Porteño." Coupled with the cobblestone streets and abundance of bars and cafes, this vibrant and distinctly bohemian neighborhood quickly became my favorite. It goes without saying that additional stops at a few of the watering holes I'd encounter along the way were essential, allowing me to soak up an extra dose of the local vibe.

Many of the destinations we visited were "must-see" on the tourist agenda and had nothing to do with food. There was, however, one stop that I found most enjoyable - a visit to a wine warehouse for a private tasting of Argentinian wines.

Our host explained that, while Argentinian Malbec is the most universally recognized, there are other varietals grown in significant volumes around the country that have not yet gained equal recognition. Along with Malbec, we sampled Chardonnay, Torrontes, Sauvignon Blanc, Syrah, and Bonarda. While Argentinian Malbec remains one of my favorites, the Bonarda (also known as Douce Noir) became my new best friend. I found its deep ruby color, medium body, low tannins, smooth finish, and notes of rich red fruit both alluring and delicious. Even today, whenever I'm buying wine, I'll look for an Argentinian Bonarda to include in my basket.

Once our group disbanded for the day, our guide went out of her way to introduce me to a large but relatively inconspicuous fast casual restaurant adjacent to the Theater District. While known for its pizza (surprisingly popular in this city), I asked about those dishes that would be considered uniquely local and a bit more adventurous.

Since they were proudly displayed in a case immediately adjacent to the front door, it was suggested that I try the empanadas. These freshly baked pastries were warm, flaky, meaty and satisfying. Seeking to experience as many of the varieties as possible, I sampled the beef, pork, cheese and chicken options, each delivering a flavor profile quite different from the others.

Having consumed a plate-load of empanadas, it was time for dessert. Considering I was looking for local delights, it was suggested that I try dulce de batata, a dense, somewhat gelatinous paste made from sweet potato. While quite unusual in both flavor and texture, and probably not appealing to everyone, this dish is a traditional Argentinian treat typically served with some form of soft white cheese at the conclusion of a meal. While I have no desire to prepare this dish at home (there are several recipes available online), I would certainly give it another try if found on a menu.

Speaking of treats, no visit to Buenos Aires is complete without dulce de leche and alfajores.

Dulce de leche, a sweet caramel spread enjoyed nationwide, is a confection made from milk, sugar and vanilla. It is enjoyed on toast for breakfast, over ice cream, with creme caramel, and even in spoonfuls straight out of the jar.

Of course, wandering the streets of Buenos Aires could never be complete without an encounter with alfajores, a delightful confection that features dulce de leche sandwiched between two delicate cookies. The dominant brand for alfajores is Havanna - omnipresent in grocery stores and gift shops as well as company owned retail outlets that are scattered around town and in the airport. It is no surprise that tourists fill their suitcases with Havanna's brightly colored boxes of alfajores as gifts for their friends and family back home. I certainly did.

Before I finish telling you about my adventures with confectionery, I would be remiss if I did not include my encounters with locally produced ice cream. To my delight, these were the thick, dense, and creamy variety known as gelati that I had learned to love while traveling in Italy. The varieties served in Buenos Aires were incredibly rich, flavor forward, and available in dulce de leche (no surprise here), dark chocolate (my favorite), chocolate & dulce de leche, and many others that were undeniably exotic. With an ice cream shop operated by Freddo (one of Argentina's better known producers) just down the street from the hotel, I managed to get away most afternoons to sample as many of their flavors as possible.

Of course, no discussion of cuisine from this part of the world would be complete without mentioning Argentinian beef. Widely recognized as some of the most tender and flavorful in the world, tourists flock to Buenos Aires in search of the perfect steak.

I must admit that, in spite of the overwhelming presence of highly regarded steakhouses throughout the city, and multiple occasions for sampling Argentinian beef, I did not find it any better than steaks from restaurants serving high quality USDA Prime beef back home. The good news is that, in every steakhouse I patronized, there was always something that captured my attention and contributed to enduring memories.

One of the most memorable experiences with Argentinian beef is based on a steak known as matambre - a cut taken from between the skin and ribs commonly referred to as the "fly shaker" (apparently, this is the muscle that allows the animal to twitch and repel flies). While similar to flank steak in shape and size, its texture is more like brisket. When tenderized with milk, grilled over hot coals, then topped with tomato sauce, fresh basil, and buffalo mozzarella, it is deliciously transformed into Matambre a la Pizza. I've endeavored to find this cut at home so that I could prepare a recipe for this book. So far, I can't seem to find anyone familiar with this particular style of beef. Apparently, it's an Argentinian specialty that has not found its way into U.S. restaurants or supermarkets.

The other steakhouse dish was not a steak at all and was not actually beef (although there may be traces of beef used in the recipe). It all started by my wanting to find an authentic Argentinian steak served in a steakhouse somewhere off the beaten path. In order to avoid the tourist-driven steakhouses, I elected to wander in and around a neighborhood popular with locals.

After about an hour, I realized that the best place I would find was the curious little steakhouse with the sausages hanging in the window that I had passed about 15 blocks and thirty minutes earlier. Unfortunately, I had no recollection of exactly where it was and was not prepared to backtrack for another hour to find it.

Becoming tired, irritable, and hungry, I decided on a place that was busy but lacked the charm and intimacy I was hoping for. It had an impressive open kitchen, lots of steaks on the grill, and a few strings of sausages hanging on the back wall. It would do.

With my limited Spanish vocabulary, I was able to understand the menu reasonably well. Since there was nothing particularly unusual or indecipherable, I started my meal with an inconsequential green salad. For my main course, however, I decided to be adventurous, ordering a plate of the sausages I had noticed earlier. The waiter said they were called "more-see-zha." All I knew is that these sausages were plump, large, darkly colored, and compelling. Since I've enjoyed every sausage that's ever crossed my lips, I expected this Argentinian variety would be equally satisfying. Guess again.

Turns out these sausages are called morcilla - a blood sausage flavored with spices including  nutmeg and cinnamon that are dry cured, then finished on the grill. When the plate arrived, the sausages were hot, firm to the touch, and looked delicious. Once sliced, however, it was apparent that they had the consistency of mashed potatoes, not at all what I had expected and unlike any sausage I had eaten before.

Not wanting to let a little unfamiliarity stand in my way, and not wanting to miss out on the experience of this local favorite, I soldiered on. While the overall flavor and char-grilled qualities were enjoyable, the texture was not. Let's just say that blood sausage, while intriguing, will not be appearing on my plate again, any time soon. Fortunately, I had ordered a bottle of Bonarda to accompany my meal and was able to wash away any lingering unpleasantness.

On the walk home, I simply prayed that the Freddo gelati store would be open.

# ROAST BRISKET
Serves 8

I've mentioned Matambre a la Pizza but have yet to find a butcher who offers this cut of beef. Since its texture is similar to brisket, I thought I'd share my recipe for Roast Brisket.

*INGREDIENTS*
16 oz. tomato puree
5 lb. brisket, trimmed of excess fat
2 onions, cut into large chunks
6 carrots, peeled
4 potatoes, peeled and quartered
3 bay leaves
1 cup water
salt and pepper

*DIRECTIONS*
Spread half of the tomato puree in the bottom of a large roasting pan. Place the brisket on top, spread the remaining puree over top, then scatter the onions, carrots, potatoes and bay leaves on top of, and around, the meat. Add the water, then sprinkle with generous amounts of salt and pepper.

Cover with foil and bake in a 375F degree oven for 4 hours.

When fully cooked, remove the brisket and allow to rest for 15 minutes, then slice thinly across the grain. To serve, place the sliced meat, potatoes, carrots and onions on a large platter.

To make a gravy, spoon off any residual fat from the drippings and transfer to a saucepan. Over medium heat, whisk in 3 tablespoons flour and 1/4 cup water and cook until thickened.

Serve with wide egg noodles or rice.

# SHRIMP EMPANADAS
## Makes 30

---

*INGREDIENTS*
Filling
2 tablespoons olive oil
1 cup onion, finely chopped
2 teaspoons garlic, minced
1 1/2 lb. tomatoes, chopped
2 bay leaves
1 lb. shrimp, cut into 1/4 inch pieces
2 tablespoons pickled jalapeños, finely chopped
1 tablespoon pickled jalapeño juice
1 tablespoon green olives, finely chopped
1 teaspoon capers, finely chopped
salt and pepper, to taste

Pastry
1 cup butter
6 oz. cream cheese
2 cups flour
1/2 teaspoon salt
1 egg, beaten (for wash)
1 tablespoon water (for wash)

*DIRECTIONS*
To make the filling, pour the olive oil into a large sauté pan. Add the onions and garlic and cook for 2 minutes. Add the tomatoes and bay leaves and continue cooking until just dry. Add the shrimp, jalapeños, olives and capers and reduce until just dry once again. Transfer the shrimp filling to a bowl, set aside, and allow to cool.

To make the pastry, place the butter and cream cheese in a large mixing bowl. Using an electric mixer, beat together until thoroughly incorporated. Mix in the flour and salt, a little at a time, kneading the ingredients together until a dough is formed. Split the dough into two balls, wrap in plastic and refrigerate for 15 minutes.

In a small bowl, beat the egg and water together and set aside.

To assemble, start by rolling out the dough, making it thin enough to handle without breaking. Using a 4-inch circular cookie cutter (or an empty can), cut the dough into circles. Place a tablespoon of filling on one half of the dough circle, brush the edges with egg wash, then fold the dough over to create a half circle filled pastry. Press the edges together with the tip of a fork to ensure a tight seal.

Bake at 375°F for 15 minutes or until golden brown. Serve warm.

---

*"He who eats alone chokes alone."*
*Arabian Proverb*

---

 A significantly more relaxed lifestyle (especially at the beach) that favors 2-wheeled beach cruisers for transportation and wardrobes pared down to nothing more than board shorts and bikinis.

I had been living in various locations in and around the Baltimore/Washington corridor for more than a decade, all a long way from the beach and a lifestyle I yearned to retrieve. Adding to my dissatisfaction was the winter of 2009 - 2010 that included one of the most severe snowstorms to hit the Mid-Atlantic states in more than 100 years. Over the course of three months, enduring a relentless series of nor'easters (affectionately called "Snowmageddon"), the region was effectively buried under a deep and heavy blanket of snow.

Under these conditions, life was brought to a standstill, my mood changed from disgust and despair to near panic, and I became increasingly claustrophobic and short of breath. Since I've never been a fan of cold weather, do not own a single sweater, and recently endured a painful divorce, it was clear that the time to clear town had arrived.

The decision to live in Jacksonville was based on several elements. Most important were those that would appeal to my hedonistic and sensory preferences (warm weather, access to good food, casual lifestyle). Equally vital was getting away from the everyday factors associated with big city living (traffic, noise, crowds, pollution).

For Jacksonville, the most compelling attributes were its proximity to the Atlantic Ocean (beach front) and a climate significantly warmer than Baltimore and the mid-Atlantic (there would no longer be a need to keep a snow shovel, windshield scraper, or a ready supply of sidewalk salt on hand). I was also impressed by its small yet efficient airport, significantly lighter traffic volumes, affordable housing, easy access to parking, beautiful waterways and park lands, frequent sightings of exotic wildlife (armadillos, manatees, herons, egrets and alligators were - and still are - the ones that impress me the most) and a significantly more relaxed lifestyle (especially at the beach) that favors 2-wheeled beach cruisers for transportation and wardrobes pared down to nothing more than board shorts and bikinis.

While I had also considered living in Santa Barbara and would have enjoyed its proximity to California's robust agricultural community, the bright lights of Los Angeles to the south, and easy access to my brother and sister-in-law just up the coast in San Francisco, I found this tony coastal community prohibitively expensive. While I had hoped to live somewhere within the city core, giving me walking access to shops, restaurants and the beach, the closest housing I could find on my budget was a drab little duplex at the city's northernmost boundary with the sole attribute of easy access to the local methadone and drug rehab clinic.

Considering that I had already lived in Southern California for 15 years, was quite familiar with its attractions (been there, done that), and the casual urban lifestyle I wanted to maintain was obviously out of my financial reach, selecting Jacksonville became an easy decision. I would also enjoy proximity to some very compelling destinations including Miami, Atlanta, Savannah, Charleston and New Orleans; offering an endless array of exciting new regional adventures and experiences.

Understanding that I am a huge fan of Southern cuisine, and knowing that shrimp & grits, biscuits & gravy, hush puppies, barbecue, macaroni & cheese, corn bread, key lime pie and pecan pie were all local favorites, and regional cuisine from this part of the world was attracting innovative new chefs and delightful new restaurants, it was highly unlikely that I would be deprived of culinary stimulation. It was also clear that I would need to find a good gym and embrace regular workouts to avoid outgrowing my wardrobe.

To kick off my Southern adventure, I signed a short-term lease for a furnished one-bedroom apartment in Jacksonville Beach, conveniently located one block from the sand. It also provided easy access to the coast highway (A1A), a nicely stocked Publix grocery store, and the east-west freeway (JTB) that would provide efficient access to interstate highways and the city's cool and groovy urban core.

Before signing, however, I made sure the kitchen had plenty of workspace, a counter top large enough to accommodate my cutting board, and sufficient room to roll out a pie crust.

Now that the decisions were made, the boxes unloaded, and Jax Beach officially my new home, it was time to go shopping. Needing a few staples for the pantry, coupled with ingredients for my first meal - I thought I'd make a relatively simple broccoli stir fry - I headed over to the Publix for my first purposeful grocery encounter.

During my exploratory visits to Jacksonville, needs from the supermarket were limited to salty snacks, cold cuts, and a few prepared foods. This time around, I needed to buy kitchen essentials including vinegar, olive oil, peanut oil, flour, onions, garlic, fresh ginger, skinless chicken breasts, and broccoli. Not surprisingly, all but the last item were easy to find and exactly what I expected.

I actually had to ask for help finding the broccoli - assistance usually required for the more ethnic or seasonal items such as tamarind, rhubarb, taro, and persimmon. With a produce clerk taking the lead, I was conducted to the furthest, darkest recesses of the produce department and introduced to veg- etables of questionable quality shrink wrapped against a purple styrofoam tray. Apparently, the idea of ice filled end caps with an abundance of crisp, fresh stalks of broccoli was more of a big city and/or Yankee thing. Now that home was far below the Mason-Dixon line, I'd have to accept these sad and forlorn veggies mercilessly entombed in a stretch-n-seal sarcophagus. And as I came to learn after numerous shopping adventures, the broccoli would not be my only disappointment.

As with my relocation to Baltimore, finding the variety of ethnic ingredients I'd need to satisfy my cooking preferences was a top priority. To my delight, I found a sizable Asian population in Jacksonville and a number of small ethnic supermarkets scattered around town that catered to these communities. While none of these stores were as well-stocked as H-Mart or Lotte Asian supermarkets in Baltimore and Northern Virginia,

I quickly found reliable access to essential shelf stable items such as Chinese soy sauce, sweet chili sauce, toasted sesame oil, rice stick, tamarind paste, sambal oelek, shrimp paste, straw mushrooms and dried shitake mushrooms. I also found fresh and refrigerated ingredients including bok choy, bean shoots, garlic chives, Chinese broccoli, bamboo shoots, Napa cabbage, ginger, Thai basil, lemongrass, tofu, dim sum and won ton wrappers, miso, curry paste, various dried seaweeds, and fish cake. While some of these ingredients could also be found in the international aisle and/or produce section at Publix or Whole Foods, the offerings at the Asian markets were in far better condition and considerably cheaper than anything these mainstream supermarkets had on hand.

Since I was eager to learn my way around town, winding my way around town in search of the city's storied watering holes was a good way to start. Without a doubt, there are a few that I discovered that continue to be my personal favorites today.

Dos Gatos, situated directly across the street from the historic Florida Theater and smack in the center of downtown Jacksonville, is a dark and mysterious place that, without a proper introduction, you could easily confuse for one of those shadier destinations frequented by career alcoholics and ne'er do wells. It is actually quite safe - patronized heavily by the cool and groovy artistic types living in and around the urban core.

From a culinary perspective, and before the idea had become a national obsession, Dos Gatos introduced creative craft cocktails to the city. If you sat at the bar long enough, you'd witness the making of all sorts of novel, distinctive, and alluring drinks. Whenever mojitos or juleps were ordered, the unmistakable aroma of muddled fresh basil and/or fresh mint with lime would waft through the room, pleasantly eliminating the lingering aromas of spilled beer (and other questionable substances).

While my preference is typically unadulterated vodka or scotch on the rocks, their eclectic variety of small batch and esoteric brands, elixirs and potions opened up new horizons for adventure and experimentation. Top shelf rums including Zacapa, Pyrat, and Diplomatico were quickly added to my vocabulary and became the spirits I would enjoy on an increasingly regular basis. I also learned about better brands of gin including Nolets and Bulldog, both now full-time inhabitants in my liquor cabinet.

While the rums are too good to insult with mixers of any kind, the gins lend a distinctive and flavorful edge when crafting cocktails such as Gin & Tonic, Gin Fizz, Gin Gimlet and/or Bijou.

The other watering hole that became an immediate favorite is the Lemon Bar, situated on the northeastern corner of Neptune Beach at the ocean's edge. It is an entirely outdoor space (a few seats at the bar are covered) that allows patrons to enjoy their favorite cocktails while taking in the sun and the sights typically associated with beach life (see wardrobe, above).

If you want to experience something a bit darker, dustier, and within spitting distance of the Lemon Bar, you can check out one of Jacksonville's oldest and most revered coastal institutions. Founded in 1933, Pete's has consistently provided adult refreshment and billiards to multiple generations of youthful hipsters, curious tourists, and well-seasoned regulars.

Due to its age, and successfully obtaining permission from the city's legislature, Pete's is one of the last remaining refuges for confirmed smokers. For me, a smoker's bar is about as attractive as open heart surgery so, aside from a few curious investigations, I have not returned. This being said, Thanksgiving at the beach would not be the same without Pete's.

Starting early in the morning on Thanksgiving Day, Pete's becomes the epicenter for a block party that attracts thousands of revelers to the corner of Lemon and First Streets. In order to accommodate the crowds, they move the bar onto the sidewalk and pour a limited menu of beer, champagne and Bloody Marys.

Even if the idea of drinking before noon is off-putting, it's worth attending at least once to watch the spectacular parade of humanity and the menagerie of pets that accompany them. People come out in droves, many sporting festive, holiday themed costumes and headdresses, all eager to share in the camaraderie that readily available cocktails and the long holiday weekend inspire. It is, without exaggeration, the party of the year. My friends and I have now attended for several years, priming ourselves with homemade Bloody Marys and some freshly baked sausage & cheddar roll-ups. With engines warmed, we happily meander up the street to embrace the festivities that await.

When it comes to local cuisine, and bearing in mind this is the South, my first restaurant meal had to be shrimp & grits. It goes without saying that I was immediately smitten by this creamy, spicy and aromatic combination of sausage, shrimp and rice. It was also quite clear that, were I to make this dish a mainstay, I would need a new wardrobe to cover the expanding waistline that would ensue. Let's just say that I moderate the frequency in which I allow myself this gastronomic delight.

The other regional staple that takes no arm twisting to consume is mac-n-cheese. While the ever-popular blue-boxed grocery variety had been a longtime favorite for years, nothing compares to the rich, sometimes spicy, configurations that can be enjoyed throughout this part of the world.

Nowadays, I make it from scratch, typically for holiday meals and other occasions when guests come over for dinner. Assuming a Rubenesque figure is not going to make a fashionable return any time soon, making mac-n-cheese on a regular basis, as with shrimp & grits, is just not in the cards.

Curiously, the longer I've lived in Jacksonville, and the more I've encountered southern regional foods, the more intrigued I've become about their origins and preparation. The upshot, and after two years of research and recipe testing, I published my second cookbook - *The First Coast Heritage Cookbook* - that describes the culinary influences in northeast Florida from 14,000BC through to 1821 (when Florida becomes a US territory).

I'm still being introduced to local favorites by the chefs and culinary enthusiasts I count as friends, as well as through local restaurants and at house parties. There's deviled eggs, pimiento cheese dip, boiled peanuts and buffalo chicken dip, plus every possible configuration of barbecue imaginable. Haven't encountered chitterlings yet but figure they are bound to turn up on my plate sooner or later.

I have every expectation that the culinary adventure in Northeast Florida, whatever the ingredients, will continue for years to come.

# BIJOU VIOLETTE
## Serves 2

---

*INGREDIENTS*
8 Griottines* cherries
2 decorative bamboo toothpicks
2 strips lemon peel
crushed ice
3 oz vodka
1 1/2 oz blue curacao

*DIRECTIONS*
Prepare the cherry garnish by skewering 4 cherries onto each of the toothpicks and set aside.

Rim each of two martini glasses with the lemon peel, then place the peel in the bottom of the glass.

Fill a cocktail shaker with crushed ice, then pour in the vodka and blue curacao. Cover and shake, then pour equally into two martini glasses.

Garnish each glass with the skewered cherries.

*\* Griottines are a brand of Morello cherries in liqueur and Kirsch. They are available online.*

# THE PERFECT BLOODY MARY
## Serves 12

---

*INGREDIENTS*

6 cups tomato juice
3 tablespoons lemon juice
2 tablespoons Worcestershire sauce
2 teaspoons horseradish, white, prepared*
1 teaspoon celery salt
1/2 teaspoon black pepper
1 bottle vodka
12 stalks celery, each appx. 6 inches long
12 thin slices of lemon

*DIRECTIONS*

Pour the tomato juice into a pitcher. Stir in the lemon juice, Worcestershire sauce, horseradish, celery salt, and black pepper, making sure all of the ingredients are thoroughly combined. Chill for at least 1 hour or overnight, allowing the flavors to blend.

To serve, fill a cocktail glass with ice. Add 1 1/2 ounces vodka, then fill with Bloody Mary mix. Stir, then garnish with a celery stalk and thin slice of lemon.

*\* Prepared horseradish is available in both white and red varieties in most supermarkets. It is typically found at the fresh seafood counter or in the refrigerated food aisle along with pickles.*

# BUFFALO CHICKEN DIP
## Serves 10

*INGREDIENTS*
2 cups roasted chicken meat, shredded
12 oz. cheddar, grated
8 oz. cream cheese
4 oz. mayonnaise
1/4 cup scallion, finely chopped
2 teaspoons Tabasco (hot sauce)
1/4 teaspoon salt, more to taste

*DIRECTIONS*
Preheat the oven to 400°F degrees.

Combine all of the ingredients in a large bowl, then transfer to an oven proof baking dish.

Place the dish in the oven and bake, uncovered, for approximately 30 minutes, until the dip is hot, bubbly and beginning to brown.

Serve hot, straight from the oven, with crackers, tortilla chips or ruffle cut potato chips.

# KILLER MACARONI & CHEESE
## Serves 10

---

*INGREDIENTS*
8 tablespoons butter, divided
1 cup onion, finely chopped
1/2 teaspoon crushed red pepper
1 clove garlic, minced
1/4 cup flour
3 cups whole milk, additional if needed
3 cups grated extra-sharp cheddar
2 cups grated Parmesan
1 cup mascarpone
salt and pepper, to taste
1 cup panko
1/2 cup chopped Italian parsley
1 pound rotelle (or elbow macaroni)

*DIRECTIONS*
Preheat the oven to 350°F.

In a 4 quart saucepan, melt 4 tablespoon butter, then sauté the onion until soft. Add the pepper and garlic and stir.

Whisk in the flour, followed by the milk, a little at a time, making sure the consistency is kept smooth. Bring to a simmer, stirring until the mixture is thick enough to coat a spoon - about 5 minutes. Remove from heat.

Stir in the cheeses, adding additional milk (if needed) to keep the sauce from getting too thick. Season with salt and pepper to taste.

In a large skillet, melt the remaining 4 tablespoons butter. Add the panko, stirring until lightly browned, then set aside. Mix in the parsley when slightly cooled.

In a separate pot, cook the pasta, until al dente. Drain thoroughly. Combine the pasta and cheese sauce together.

Grease a 9" x 13" baking pan. Pour in the pasta mixture and spread evenly. Sprinkle the panko mixture over top, distributing evenly across the surface.

Bake 350°F for 30 minutes or until top is nicely browned. Serve immediately.

NOTE: This recipe is best served freshly made and straight from the oven.

---

*"Food is our common ground,*
*a universal experience."*
*James Beard*

---

# SAUSAGE & CHEDDAR BISCUIT ROLL-UPS
### Makes 16 Rollups

---

*INGREDIENTS*

1 leek
1/2 lb breakfast sausage (casings removed)
1/2 lb sharp cheddar cheese, grated
2 cups flour
1 teaspoon baking powder
1/2 teaspoon baking soda
1/2 teaspoon salt
1/2 cup butter (cold, cut into small pieces)
3/4 cup buttermilk
1 egg, beaten (for sealing the rollups)

*DIRECTIONS*

To prepare the filling: Cut the leek in half lengthwise and again in half crosswise. Wash thoroughly under cold water to remove all of the grit, then drain and pat dry with a towel. Cut into thin slices and set aside.

Cook the sausage meat over medium heat, breaking up large clumps to create a fine crumble texture. Carefully transfer the cooked sausage crumble into a small bowl, keeping the drippings in the pan.

Using the same pan and reserved sausage drippings, saute the sliced leeks until soft. Carefully drain and transfer the leeks to a small bowl.

To make the dough: Mix the flour, baking powder, baking soda and salt together in a large bowl. Using a fork, cut in the butter until the flour is crumbly. Add the buttermilk, a little at a time, to form a dough. Divide the dough in half and form two balls.

To assemble: When you are ready with the fillings and dough, preheat the oven to 375°F.

Roll one of the dough balls on a floured board to achieve a thin pastry approximately 10 inches x 10 inches. Trim any irregular edges, as needed, to make a perfect square.

Sprinkle half of the cooked leeks, sausage and cheese evenly across the dough, leaving the first and last inch of the dough clear of topping.

Gently lift the edge closest to you and begin rolling, taking care not to puncture the dough. When you get to the last inch, brush the dough with egg wash, then roll up completely. The egg will seal the roll.

Trim off any loose bits at each end of the roll, then cut into 8 even pieces.

Place each of the slices into a prepared muffin pan (you may prefer to use muffin wrappers).

Repeat the process with the second ball of dough, then bake for 15 - 20 minutes until nicely browned. Allow to cool slightly, then transfer to a clean plate and serve.

# SHRIMP & GRITS
## Serves 4

---

*INGREDIENTS*
Make the Filling
1 tablespoon butter
4 cloves garlic, minced
1/4 cup shallots, finely chopped
1/4 lb. ham, diced
1/4 lb. andouille sausage, thinly sliced
1/4 cup tomatoes, diced
20 large shrimp, peeled and cleaned
salt, to taste
Tabasco, to taste

Make the Grits
4 cups water
1 cup grits
1/4 cup cream
1 tablespoon butter
salt and pepper, to taste

DIRECTIONS
Melt the butter in a large pan, then sauté the garlic and shallots until soft. Add the ham and sausage and continue cooking until nicely browned. Mix in the tomatoes and shrimp, cooking for 5 more minutes. Add salt and Tabasco, to taste.

To make the grits, bring the water to a boil. Stir in the grits, then cover and simmer until thick, about 10 minutes. When done, stir in the cream and butter. Add salt and pepper, to taste.

To serve, spoon some of the grits onto each plate, followed by the shrimp mixture.

AFRICA

We could see fishermen at work, an occasional hippopotamus lifting its sizable head out of the water, and colonies of cat-sized fruit bats circling the city as the sun went down.

**W**ith little more than a few Tarzan movies and dog-eared issues of National Geographic as reference, I was minimally prepared to work in Africa. As with other assignments, I knew that I would be picked up at the airport, provided adequate hotel accommodations, and fully briefed after I had settled in. I also knew that I would need to check out travel advisories and seek out appropriate vaccines and medicines. Based on my previous assignments, this was the routine I had learned to expect.

Working on an entirely different continent meant that I had to prepare myself for conditions unlike any I had encountered before. From a health and wellness perspective, my doctor recommended I make an appointment with a travel doctor to obtain inoculations and prescriptions for this part of the world. Having become accustomed to occasional aches, pains and discomforts while on assignment, I didn't give travel related medical issues that much thought. To my surprise, I soon learned that I would need a host of preventatives.

To start, there were the routine vaccinations that included measles-mumps-rubella (MMR), diphtheria-tetanus-pertussis, varicella (chickenpox), polio, and flu shot. In addition, many African nations will not let you enter without proof of vaccination for Yellow Fever so that was added to the list. Plus, I needed to be vaccinated for Hepatitis A, Typhoid, Rabies, and Meningitis. To say the least, I have never seen so many needles lined up on a tray or received so many injections up and down both arms in one session. I would also be given a prescription for malaria - tablets that I would have to take on a daily basis for the duration of my travel - as well as a cornucopia of curatives for gastro-intestinal and other such travel induced discomforts. Before I had even stepped foot on the continent, my working in Africa had already provided a truly remarkable and indelible memory.

## GHANA

My first assignment took me to Ghana's capital city of Accra. Apart from the usual differences in terms of roadways, signage, and architecture, I had not anticipated the inescapable traffic. This, along with the cacophony of car horns, rumbling engines, plumes of exhaust, and variety of questionable scents that perfumed the air, my senses were well and truly overwhelmed.

The other noteworthy difference was fashion. Although men would wear traditional African shirts from time to time, and some favored modest Islamic tunics, their garb was, for the most part, unremarkable. The women, however, were striking in their vividly colored and ornately patterned dresses, pants, and hats, all of which rivaled the most fanciful of peacocks. Considering my love of bright rainbow hues and intricate patterns, I had to make sure my staring out of admiration would not be inadvertently perceived as rude. I also had to maintain a watchful eye on where I was going. After all, every step was a new adventure.

Of course, I eagerly anticipated sampling the local cuisine and the surprises that were sure to happen. Based on preliminary research, I learned about Fufu (a dough ball made from cassava and plantains), Palaver Sauce (fish stew), and Jollof Rice (fried rice) and understood that goat, chicken and fish would be prevalent in many of the dishes I encountered.

While the hotels I stayed at were clean, modern, and well looked after, their culinary options were unremarkable - catering primarily to the inexperienced palate of foreigners. That being said, their menus always featured "local" dishes, all of which I made a point of sampling.

In Accra, there were two exceptionally satisfying and memorable meals. The first introduced me to the highly regarded Senegalese fish stew called Thieboudienne (pronounced cheh-boo-jen). Served with rice, it reminded me of a cross between a Spanish influenced Paella and a Creole influenced Étouffée.

The second dish that captured my attention was Palaver Sauce - a traditional Ghanaian stew consisting of meat, fish and leafy vegetables. Since the greatest compliment I can make when it comes to food is to find the recipe and prepare the dish at home, I have managed to find enough references to pull together my own version of Palaver Sauce. I am reasonably sure, however, there are ingredients indigenous to Ghana that have been omitted and my version is nowhere near as good.

Even today, Palaver Sauce is still a worthwhile and enjoyable dish that stirs up fond memories. While Thieboudienne was equally enjoyable, my attempts at making it have been less than wonderful. After referencing myriad recipes and attempting this dish on multiple occasions with dismal outcomes, I have decided that Senegalese cooks know something that I do not.

The most remarkable Ghanaian meal, however, took place in a small local restaurant (actually the front porch of the restaurateur's home) in the rural inland town of Ejura. Ordered by my colleagues, I enjoyed a traditional stew of goat, chicken and fish. What I found most delightful was having a truly authentic Ghanaian experience that included tableside visits from free roaming chickens, goats and the occasional house cat.

My experiences in Ghana, both cultural and culinary, prepared me for everything I would subsequently encounter in other countries on the continent. With a basic understanding and familiarity of African surroundings, and apart from safety precautions that were always a priority, it became far easier to have meaningful adventures in other places.

## BURKINA FASO

On all of my African assignments, I was advised to avoid local tap water and remain guarded about the cleanliness of restaurants. While working in Ouagadougou, the capital of Burkina Faso, I took heed and only ate at those restaurants that colleagues indicated would be safe. Sticking to the places they recommended, I was able to enjoy a variety of dishes, the most uniquely African being poulet bicyclette and the most flavorful being an Indian curry - chicken tikka massala.

Poulet bicyclette is named for the curious peddling motion that the local chickens display while walking about. While this dish was memorable, it was not due to the chicken (it had far too many bones and not enough meat). What caught my attention was the sweet corn salad that was served as the accompanying side dish. A relatively simple mix of corn, tomatoes and red onion, this salad was a wonderfully cool and an incredibly fresh contrast to the grilled chicken.

The chicken tikka massala was just one of many dishes I enjoyed at Namastae India, one of the best Indian restaurants in Ouaga. While my exposure to Indian food in the past had been limited and not terribly favorable, the variety of curries, breads and salads that I experienced at Namaste were truly remarkable. Needless to say, and whenever possible, I made a concerted effort to return and work my way through their menu. Even today, Indian food continues to be one of my most favorite ethnic cuisines.

## NIGER

While working in Burkina Faso, I also delivered presentations and consulted with food producers in the neighboring country of Niger. In order to get into the capital city of Niamey by road, our driver took us onto a bridge that spanned the Niger River. As we crossed this mid-sized waterway, we could see fishermen at work as well as an occasional hippopotamus lifting its sizable head out of the water. Coupled with colonies of cat-sized fruit bats that regularly circled the city as the sun went down, I kept busy scanning the surface of the river and the skies overhead for unusual signs of life.

From a culinary perspective, what I enjoyed most were the deliciously marinated beef kabobs served hot off the grill during happy hour at my hotel's poolside bar. Served with little mounds of Dijon mustard, peri peri sauce and an African peanut spice, these flavorful barbecued treats were eagerly anticipated, along with my usual Scotch on the rocks every day after work.

I was also delighted to learn that the popularity of Indian food was not limited to Burkina Faso. In Niger, a sister Namastae India restaurant was operating in Niamey and not far from my hotel. Realizing that I could safely continue my exploration of Indian cuisine, I sampled and came to love all sorts of intriguing and richly spiced dishes including goat rogan josh, lamb korma, and paneer makhani.

### MALAWI

My work in the sub-Saharan west African nations of Ghana, Burkina Faso and Niger was followed by several assignments in Malawi, located in the southeastern part of the continent. Spread over several years, the experiences in the capital city of Lilongwe and surrounding areas, coupled with some of the relationships that were forged, were some of the most re-markable and cherished to date.

As with other travel destinations, food safety in and around Lilongwe remained a significant concern. As such, based on recommendations from other expats working in the region, I was given a relatively short list of restaurants that were considered worthwhile and worry free. Not surprisingly, several of these recommendations were Indian restaurants, allowing me to continue my decidedly delicious education associated with Indian cuisine. I basically started at the top of the menu and, from day to day, ordered my way down their list of offerings including a variety of breads (naan, roti and kulcha), biryani (featuring chicken, mutton or prawns), and an endless assortment of curries.

When it came to local foods, primarily due to concerns about food safety, my encounters were extremely limited. No matter how appealing a restaurant, cafe or street vendor, the risk of illness far outweighed my curiosity and hunger. That being said, I did enjoy a few meals that featured locally harvested tilapia from Lake Malawi and a few vegetarian dishes that made wonderful use of cassava and sweet potato. Of note was a spicy dish made with leafy greens. After receiving assistance with the local language (chefs did not speak English - only Chichewa), I learned this particular dish featured mustard greens, a popular Malawian staple. With the addition of onion, tomato and a little bit of chili, the end result was undeniably delicious.

I would regularly travel significant distances to meet with food growers and processors at their farms and offices. While driving, we would encounter enterprising young men along the road selling snacks, bottled water, and other such impulse items. Of note were the vendors holding up long sticks, several in each hand. When passing by at high speeds, it was hard to see what they held. Upon careful inspection, it became obvious that these sticks were actually long barbecue skewers, each with 6 to 8 small grilled field mice. Apparently, Malawians enjoy mice that have been grilled dry in the same manner Americans enjoy jerky.

I noticed other roadside hawkers holding up what looked like large balls of cotton candy on a stick. These turned out to be roadside snacks covered with a small white plastic bag that kept the bugs away. When the bag was removed, skewers of grilled meat would be revealed, this time, the sticks held 6 to 8 tiny grilled bird carcasses. Having never seen such tiny birds (they were not more than an inch or so in length, reminding me of mini roast turkeys with legs and wings attached), I learned they were called Elbee Jays. It was subsequently revealed that I had misunderstood. These were a non-specific variety of bird simply known as L-B-Js - Little Brown Jobs.

Since cooking conditions in these smaller villages was questionable, and I was not acclimated to local food and water, I passed on the opportunity to sample the mice and birds. I must admit, I don't believe I missed anything.

## SOUTH AFRICA

Although I never had reason to step foot into South Africa other than to make airline connections in Johannesburg, my work on the continent brought me into contact with a number of South African expats. When I would describe my culinary adventures on the continent, they would always recommend South African biltong - spiced and dried meat strips similar to jerky. I was also told about a curiously named dish called bunny chow.

Biltong was sold in many of the convenience stores throughout the Johannesburg airport, making it easy to sample this particular snack. Knowing that better quality versions and a broader variety of flavor options would probably be available in supermarkets or local grocery stores, I would have to make do with whatever I could find. As with jerky, it was meaty and chewy with a slightly different texture. The spices were undeniably exotic. What they were remains a mystery... for now.

Bunny chow, not surprisingly, was not something I would find in the airport. Apparently, it is a specialty that originated among the Indian population in the coastal town of Durban. Based on my research, it is essentially a hollowed out loaf of bread filled with curry. While I have found a perfectly acceptable recipe for bunny chow that I make at home, I am eager to visit Durban and sample the real thing.

# BEEF KEBABS WITH PEANUT SPICE *(NIGER)*
### Serves 4 - 6

These kebabs were prepared every evening on the outdoor patio overlooking the Niger River at the Grand Hotel in Niamey. While I'm sure the chef thought I was a silly tourist, I learned about the ingredients and was able to formulate this recipe after I returned home. While I cannot watch for hippos or fruit bats at sunset, I still enjoy this dish whenever I fire up the grill at home.

*INGREDIENTS*
1/2 cup soy sauce
1/2 cup mirin
6 tablespoons sugar
2 tablespoons garlic, minced
1 tablespoon sesame oil
2 lb. flank steak, cut into 3/4" cubes
12 skewers (if wood, soaked in water for at least 6 to 8 hours)

Peanut Spice
1 cup peanuts, unsalted
1 teaspoon garlic powder
1 teaspoon sweet paprika

For Dipping
Dijon mustard
Peri Peri sauce (available from most gourmet stores)

*DIRECTIONS*
In a large bowl, combine the soy, mirin, sugar, garlic and oil. Mix in the steak cubes, making sure the meat is completely covered with marinade. Cover and refrigerate for 6 to 8 hours, stirring the meat every couple of hours.

To make peanut spice, place a small quantity of peanuts in a coffee mill. Grind in brief pulses to achieve a consistency similar to coarse cornmeal. (Note: lengthy or excessive grinding will yield an unwanted pasty consistency). Sift or strain the peanut powder to remove large chunks. After all of the peanuts have been ground, mix the peanut powder with garlic and paprika.

To cook the kebabs, place meat cubes on prepared skewers and grill over a hot charcoal fire, cooking to desired level of doneness (medium rare is recommended).

Serve the grilled kebabs with small portions of Peanut Spice, Dijon and Peri Peri for dipping.

---

*"We must have a pie. Stress cannot exist in the presence of a pie."*
*David Mamet*

---

# CHARGRILLED MOUSE *(MALAWI)*
## Serves 6

---

*INGREDIENTS*
3 tablespoons soy sauce
3 tablespoons Asian sesame oil
2 tablespoons rice wine vinegar
1 tablespoon chili garlic sauce
1 1/2 lb. chicken tenders
1/2 lime

*DIRECTIONS*
In a small bowl, combine the soy, sesame oil, vinegar and chili garlic sauce and set aside.

Using a fork, pierce each piece of chicken on all sides, then place in the bottom of a flat dish. Pour the marinade over the chicken, making sure to coat each piece completely on all sides. Cover and refrigerate for 30 minutes. Turn the chicken pieces, re-distribute the marinade, cover and refrigerate for an additional 30 minutes.

Place the marinated chicken on a hot grill* and cook for 7 minutes. Turn the chicken over once and cook for another 7 minutes. When done, remove from the grill, squeeze lime juice over top and serve.

* You may find it helpful to place the chicken on skewers before grilling, making it easier to handle over a hot flame.

# CHICKEN KORMA *(NIGER)*
### Serves 8

---

*INGREDIENTS*
1 onion, coarsely chopped
4 garlic cloves, coarsely chopped
2 tablespoons ginger, coarsely chopped
2 bay leaves, crumbled
4 cardamom pods, crushed, seeds extracted  (no more)
4 cloves, whole  (no more)
4 tablespoons peanut oil
1 teaspoon cumin
1/2 teaspoon garam masala
1/2 teaspoon coriander
1/2 teaspoon cinnamon
1/4 teaspoon red pepper flakes
3/4 cup cream
1/2 cup coconut milk
2 tablespoons almond flour
2 tablespoons brown sugar
2 tablespoons lemon juice
1 tablespoon tomato paste
1 1/4 tsp salt
2 lb chicken, cut into 1/2-inch strips
coriander leaves, chopped - for garnish

*DIRECTIONS*
Put the onion, garlic, ginger, bay leaves, cardamom and cloves into a blender to make a smooth paste (add a little water if needed). Set aside.

Heat the oil in a Dutch oven over a high flame. Add the onion, garlic and ginger paste and cook for several minutes.

Add the cumin, garam masala, coriander, cinnamon and pepper and stir, making sure the spices are fully incorporated. Cook for about 5 minutes, then stir in the cream, coconut milk, almond flour, brown sugar, lemon juice, tomato paste, and salt. Continue cooking until all of the ingredients are fully incorporated and begin to bubble. Adjust seasoning to taste, as needed.

Add the chicken, making sure it is fully coated by the sauce. Cover and simmer for 20 minutes, stirring occasionally until the chicken is fully cooked.

Serve with cooked Jasmine or Basmati rice topped with the chicken and plenty of sauce. Garnish with fresh coriander.

---

*"Why don't cannibals eat clowns?*
*They taste funny."*
*Unknown*

---

# CHICKEN TIKKA MASALA  *(BURKINA FASO)*
### Serves 6

---

*INGREDIENTS*
<u>Chicken Marinade</u>
3/4 cup yogurt (whole milk, not Greek)
1 tablespoon peanut oil
1/2 lime, juiced
2 cloves garlic, crushed
2 lb. boneless chicken breasts, cut lengthwise into 1"

<u>Sauce</u>
6 garlic cloves, finely grated
1 tablespoon grated ginger
4 teaspoons ground turmeric
2 teaspoons garam masala
2 teaspoons ground coriander
2 teaspoons ground cumin
1/2 teaspoon cayenne
3 tablespoons vegetable oil
1 cup onion, finely chopped
8 cardamom pods (seeds only, shells discarded)
1/4 cup tomato paste
1 28-ounce can crushed tomatoes
1 1/2 cups heavy cream
3/4 cup fresh cilantro, chopped (more for garnish)
salt, to taste
Steamed basmati rice (for serving)

*DIRECTIONS*
In a large bowl, whisk together the yogurt, oil, lime juice and garlic. Add the chicken, making sure to fully coat each strip. Cover and marinate in the refrigerator for 1 hour.

In a small bowl, combine the garlic, ginger, turmeric, garam masala, coriander, cumin and cayenne.

Heat the oil in a large pot or Dutch oven. Stir in the onion and cardamom seeds and saute for about 5 minutes or until the onions are soft. Add the tomato paste and cook for another 5 minutes, stirring frequently to avoid burning. Add the spice mixture and continue cooking until the bottom of pot begins to brown.

Add the tomatoes, bring to a boil, then simmer for 10 minutes, allowing all of the ingredients to blend.

Add the cream and cilantro and simmer for another 20 minutes, stirring occasionally to prevent sticking or burning.

Preheat the broiler. Place the chicken in an oven-proof dish and broil, uncovered, for about 10 minutes. When cooked, remove from oven, cut into bite-size pieces and add to sauce. Simmer for another 5 minutes.

Serve over rice. Garnish with fresh cilantro.

# FISH WITH SPINACH PALAVER SAUCE *(GHANA)*
## Serves 4

---

*INGREDIENTS*
2 tablespoons olive oil
2 cups onions, finely chopped
1 1/2 cups fish stock
1 lb fresh spinach, chopped
2 cups fresh tomatoes, chopped
1/2 cup okra, thinly sliced
1 teaspoon salt
1/2 teaspoon crushed red pepper
1/2 teaspoon black pepper
1 cup pumpkin seeds, shelled, toasted and ground
1 tablespoon ginger, grated
1 lb. Red Snapper (or other firm white fish)
1/2 lb. shrimp (21-25 count)

*DIRECTIONS*
*Place a large Dutch oven over medium high heat. Add the oil, stir in the onions, and cook for about 5 minutes.*

*Add the stock and bring to a boil, then reduce to a simmer. Stir in the spinach, then the tomatoes, okra, salt, red pepper, and black pepper. Cook over low heat for 15 minutes.*

*Add the ground pumpkin seeds and ginger, stirring often, and cook until a thick, sauce-like consistency is achieved.*

*Add the fish and cook for 5 minutes. Add the shrimp and continue until all of the seafood is fully cooked.*

*Add salt and pepper, as needed, to taste.*

*Serve immediately over a bed of rice.*

# SPICY MUSTARD GREENS  (MALAWI)
## Serves 4

*INGREDIENTS*
3 tablespoons sunflower oil
1 cup onion, finely chopped
1 serrano chili, finely chopped
1 lb. mustard greens, coarsely chopped
2 cups tomato, coarsely chopped
salt and pepper, to taste

*DIRECTIONS*
*Place the oil in the bottom of a large skillet over medium high heat. Add the onion and sauté until soft, about 5 minutes. Add the chili and mustard greens and toss. Continue cooking until greens begin to soften. Add the tomatoes and cook for another 5 minutes.*

*Add salt and pepper to taste. Serve immediately*

*"Great food is like great sex.
The more you have the more you want."
Gael Greene*

# SWEET CORN & TOMATO SALAD  *(BURKINA FASO)*
### Serves 8

_____

*INGREDIENTS*
2 lb. kernel corn
1 1/2 cups tomatoes, diced
1/2 cup red onion, sliced razor thin
1 cup green onion, finely chopped
1 cup cilantro, finely chopped
2 limes, juiced
1/3 cup rice vinegar
Salt, to taste

*DIRECTIONS*
*Mix the corn, tomatoes, red and green onions and cilantro together in a large bowl. Stir in the lime juice and rice vinegar. Add salt, to taste.*

*Refrigerate for 4-6 hours. Mix once again before serving, adjusting flavors as needed.*

*NOTE: This dish goes great with grilled meats of all description.*

**LEBANON**  In very short time,
wine and arak were
served along with a steady stream
of small plates bearing a dizzying
variety of traditional foods. I tried
them all, taking care not to appear
too ravenous, gluttonous or greedy.

# LEBANON

Like most of the countries I've visited and worked, my first engagement in Lebanon would offer an array of new and exciting experiences unlike any so far. Due primarily to political instability inside the country, and military activity taking place just a short distance across their border into Syria, I expected to find a place where travel would be difficult, the environment foreboding, and the politics of the day making it difficult for me, as an outsider, to get around safely.

Since I never minimize travel advisories and am always cautious, I had planned to limit my adventures to the confines of the hotel and/or anywhere work would take me. Fortunately, my colleagues were eager to show me around Beirut and the surrounding countryside, including a drive along the Mediterranean coastline to Byblos (one of the oldest continuously inhabited cities in the world). With their help, I did not need to worry about getting lost in the wrong neighborhoods or my inability to speak the local language. The best part was seeing the pride they took showing me local sights, taking me to restaurants, and introducing me to an incredible variety of Lebanese foods.

Probably the most memorable and overwhelmingly impressive experience was the culinary phenomenon know as mezze - a shared meal consisting of a large number of hot and cold dishes served as small plates including traditional favorites such as hummus (chickpeas and tahini spread), baba ganoush (eggplant and tahini spread), sudjuk (spicy lamb sausages), falafel (mashed chickpea fritters), kibbe (minced meat quenelles with bulgur wheat and spices), and tabbouleh (a salad made with bulgur wheat, tomato, onion, and parsley), all served with baskets overflowing with freshly baked pita. No matter where the mezze took place, at the family table or in restaurants, there would always be an astonishing number of dishes to explore, taste, and enjoy for hours.

One of the most remarkable foods was an intensely flavorful condiment called toum - a spreadable emulsion made from garlic and oil. Guaranteed to scare off vampires, this creamy, brilliantly white substance is wonderful when eaten with pita as well as an accompaniment to grilled chicken and shawarma (typically spit-roasted lamb). While I have yet to make it for myself, it is one of those uniquely Lebanese foods that I came to adore from the very first bite.

Of course, no mezze was complete without a glass of Lebanese arak, an anise flavored, grape-based spirit similar to Greek ouzo, French pastis, and Turkish raki. Served over ice, one part arak to two parts water, I marveled at the way the clear arak would magically turn milky white as water was added. Out of all of the edible substances I would encounter in Lebanon, arak was the most distinctive. Ever since, no matter the occasion, enjoying a glass of arak immediately transports me back to Beirut and provokes a flood of fond memories.

Before this visit, I had heard about za'atar (or za'atar) but did not know exactly what it was or how to incorporate it into cooking. In Lebanon, and throughout the middle east, it is a common and liberally used spice blend sprinkled over, or incorporated into, both hot and cold dishes such as hummus, lebneh (thick yogurt), cooked vegetables, and roasted meats. Depending whether it is home made or commercially blended, it is made with varying proportions of thyme, oregano, marjoram, and sesame seeds and could also include a variety of other ingredients including sumac, salt, and wheat.

The most ubiquitous dish made with za'atar is man'oushe (also manakeesh), the Lebanese equivalent of pizza. Dough is rolled thin, brushed with olive oil, topped with a generous sprinkling of za'atar and baked. While it is also made with toppings such as ground meat, feta cheese, fresh herbs, cucumber, and tomato, the version I encountered most frequently in bakeries, roadside cafes, and restaurants was made simply with za'atar.

One other item that I would be remiss not to mention is the hookah. While I was first introduced to this multi-stemmed waterpipe by the caterpillar in Lewis Carrol's "Alice's Adventures in Wonderland," and I'd gain a little first-hand experience with various substances during my college years, these precedents did not adequately prepare me for what I witnessed in Lebanon.

While I do not recall the name of the neighborhood, it was clear this was one of Beirut's premier entertainment districts.

The streets were lined with restaurants and clubs, many of them large, two story affairs that offered both food and live music. In the place we visited, the downstairs was a relaxing cafe environment where patrons sipped coffee and cocktails and enjoyed casual meals. While it looked wonderful, and I would have been happy to sit and sip for a while, I quickly learned that my hosts favored the dining room on the second floor.

As soon as we walked in, I immediately understood their preference. The upstairs was a large, cavernous hall filled with long rows of communally shared tables. Waiters were busily conveying trays laden with foods and drinks of every possible description, clearing tables of plates and glasses that had been joyfully emptied, and doing everything they could to ensure their guests were well looked after.

At the same time, a two-man band was onstage at the front of the room, playing small, pear shaped guitars that I can only assume were lutes or other such Lebanese stringed instruments. Between the revelry of the patrons, the music being played, and the clatter of the dishes, the room was alive.

Seeking to minimize the cacophony, we elected to sit as far away as possible from the stage, allowing us to take in all of the festivities while, at the same time, making it a bit easier to engage in conversation. Being more than a bit distracted by this carnival of Lebanese delights, I failed to notice that food and drinks for our table had been ordered. In very short time, wine, arak and water were served along with a steady stream of small plates bearing a dizzying variety of traditional Lebanese foods. Some I recognized. Some I didn't. I tried them all enthusiastically, taking care not to appear too ravenous, gluttonous or greedy.

While all of this was taking place, there was one very tall, very thin, and quite animated server who would scurry up and down between the rows of tables, ferrying in hookahs, loading them with hot coals and tobacco, and getting patrons properly situated with a hose and mouthpiece. When he was not actually serving, he would prance and dance up and down the aisles, grinning gleefully, using the tongs meant for handling hot coals as a rhythm device, waving them around in the air while rattling them in time with the music. It goes without saying that he was as much of the show as the band and as memorable as the food.

Seeking to introduce me to as many Lebanese delights as possible, my hosts made sure a hookah was brought to our table, hoses and mouthpieces passed around, and the fire lit. As the music played, coupled with all of the other the exotic flavors, textures, sights and sounds, we would happily puff away, enjoying the warmth associated with a meal happily shared among friends. It does not get any better than this.

Sadly, my visit to Lebanon was brief, minimizing the number and variety of culinary adventures. If all goes well, I will have an opportunity to return, dig deeper, experience more, and share these adventures with you.

# BUTTERMILK CHICKEN WITH ZA'ATAR
### Serves 4

---

*INGREDIENTS*
4 chicken breast halves
2 tablespoons za'atar
1 tablespoon salt
1 1/2 tablespoons garlic, minced
1 1/2 cups buttermilk
fresh thyme sprigs

*DIRECTIONS*
Season the chicken on all sides with za'atar and salt, dividing it evenly between all four pieces.

Sprinkle half of the garlic onto the bottom of a casserole (large enough to fit the chicken in one layer). Place the chicken on top, then sprinkle with the remaining garlic. Cover the chicken with buttermilk until it is just covered (the amount used will vary, depending on the size of the breasts and the dish used for baking), then top with a few sprigs of thyme.

Cover and refrigerate for 12 hours.

Preheat the oven to 375°F.

Remove the chicken from the fridge about 1 hour prior to baking, allowing it to reach room temperature. Bake the chicken, uncovered, on the top rack in the oven for 20 minutes, then turn the oven up to broil. Cook for another 10 minutes, ensuring the chicken is nicely browned and caramelized.

Remove from the oven and serve over rice or quinoa.

# FALAFEL
Makes 12 patties

---

*INGREDIENTS*

15 oz. chickpeas (1 can), drained
1 cup onion, coarsely chopped
2 tablespoons parsley, finely chopped
2 tablespoons cilantro, finely chopped
1 tablespoon garlic, minced
1 teaspoon salt
1 teaspoon cumin
1 teaspoon baking powder
1/2 teaspoon crushed red pepper
6 tablespoons flour
vegetable oil, for frying
1 cup tomato, chopped, for garnish
2 cups lettuce, shredded, for garnish

*DIRECTIONS*

Using a food processor, combine the chickpeas, onions, parsley, cilantro, garlic, salt, cumin, baking powder and red pepper. Pulse in the flour, a little at a time, to produce a dough. Transfer the dough to a bowl, then cover and refrigerate for at least 12 hours.

To make the falafel, roll the dough into 1 1/2 inch balls, then flatten slightly to make patties.

Pour a thin layer of vegetable oil onto the bottom of a sauté pan. Over medium high heat, fry each of the patties until browned, then turn over and brown the second side. When done, transfer to paper towels and allow to drain.

Serve the falafels warm, on a platter of shredded lettuce and chopped tomatoes. Drizzle either Falafel Sauce or Tzatziki over top, just before serving.

FALAFEL SAUCE
Combine 1 cup Greek yogurt, 1/2 tablespoon lemon zest, the juice of 1/2 lemon, 1 tablespoon freshly chopped cilantro, 2 teaspoons freshly chopped parsley, 1/2 teaspoon cumin, and salt, to taste. Refrigerate for 6 hours. Adjust the flavor before serving, if needed. Keep refrigerated.

TZATZIKI
Place 16 ounces Greek yogurt, 1/2 cup peeled, seeded, and coarsely chopped cucumber, 1 tablespoon olive oil, 1 table-spoon lemon juice, 1 teaspoon minced garlic, and 1 teaspoon dried dill in a blender. Liquify the ingredients, then transfer to a bowl, cover and refrigerate for at least 1 hour. Add salt and pepper, to taste, before serving.

---

*"Seize the moment. Remember all those women on the Titanic who waved off the dessert cart."*
*Erma Bombeck*

---

# LEBANESE HUMMUS
## Serves 8

---

*INGREDIENTS*

15 oz. chickpeas (1 can), drained
1/4 cup olive oil
1/3 cup tahini
2 cloves garlic, minced
1 lemon, zested and juiced
1/2 teaspoon salt
1/2 teaspoon sumac, for garnish

*DIRECTIONS*

Using a food processor, combine the chickpeas, olive oil, tahini, garlic, zest, juice and salt. Continue processing until everything is thoroughly combined and smooth. Add water, as needed, to ensure the desired consistency.

Add additional salt, lemon juice or olive oil, to taste, as desired.

To serve, drizzle with extra olive oil and a sprinkle of sumac.

# BLACK BEAN HUMMUS
## Serves 8

*INGREDIENTS*
15 oz. black beans (1 can), drained
2 tablespoons olive oil
1/2 cup tahini
2 cloves garlic, minced
1/4 cup cilantro, chopped
3 green onions, chopped
1 teaspoon cumin
1/4 teaspoon cayenne
salt, to taste

*DIRECTIONS*
Using a food processor, combine the beans, olive oil, tahini, garlic, cilantro, onions, cumin and cayenne. Continue processing until everything is thoroughly combined and smooth. Add water, as needed, to ensure the desired consistency. Add salt to taste.

## HUMMUS WITH PEPPADEW AND RED PEPPERS
### Serves 8

*INGREDIENTS*
15 oz. chickpeas (1 can), drained
3 tablespoons olive oil
2 tablespoons tahini
2 cloves garlic, minced
1 lemon, juiced
1/2 teaspoon salt
1 roasted red pepper
6 Peppadew peppers
1/2 teaspoon za'atar

*DIRECTIONS*
Using a food processor, combine the chickpeas, olive oil, tahini, garlic, lemon juice, salt, peppers and za'atar. Continue processing until everything is thoroughly combined and smooth. Add water, as needed, to ensure the desired consistency. Add salt or za'atar to taste.

 Every morsel of food, whether a casual snack, sit down meal, or specialty of the house, was worthy of investigation. Everything was an exotic and flavorful adventure that captivated my senses.

**W**hile working in Russia, I had heard about Georgia but had no idea where it was. I was clueless about its considerable history, its ties to the Soviet Union, or what the overall look and feel of the place might be like. I had certainly never heard of foods such as khachapuri, chakhokbili, prasi, or churchkiella, and had no idea where places like Tbilisi, Kutaisi, or Batumi would be found on a map. As far as I knew, Georgia was just north of Florida, famous for its peaches and peanuts.

Having worked in Georgia on multiple occasions, my visits were always eagerly anticipated and exciting. With a base of operation in the capital city of Tbilisi, I had easy access to a place that was thousands of years old and, at the same time, quite vibrant and contemporary.

Recognizing that Georgia shares its northern border with Russia and is geographically situated at the crossroads of the storied Silk Road, the cultural and culinary influences I experienced were remarkable. While I expected Georgian cuisine would be similar to some of the dishes I enjoyed in Moscow and Stavropol, I found it had a character that was altogether different and remarkably delicious.

It all started with the ubiquitous Georgian cheese bread known as khachapuri - somewhat like a thin, cheese filled pizza dough or focaccia. Throughout the country, from supermarkets, convenience stores, and bakeries to fast casual and fine dining restaurants, there was always some form of khachapuri available.

While pursuing this cheesy delight, I quickly learned there are variations on the basic theme that are regionally influenced. This means that in some places the bread might be round, in others rectangular. The flour used in the dough varied and, depending on the style of locally produced cheese, the overall flavor and texture could be dramatically different - sometimes soft and doughy, other times light and flaky. While I have yet to work out all the regional or culinary variations, every khachapuri that has crossed my lips has always been welcomed and incredibly delicious.

Equally popular are Georgian wines. When you consider that Georgians have been engaged in winemaking for somewhere around 8,000 years, it's not surprising that so much of their production is well regarded. While I have yet to find a favorite, the adventure associated with wine tasting, sharing of bottles, and discovery continues.

As long as I am on the subject of alcoholic beverages, it seems the tradition of hospitality and the offer of a welcoming drink, similar to other countries throughout Eastern Europe, is alive and well in Georgia. Whether I was meeting with clients at their office, sharing a meal at restaurants, or attending special events, inevitably a bottle of home made wine, brandy, or both would find its way onto the table. Along with this gesture of generosity and friendship, there was an obvious pride on the part of the producer when sharing his creations. While all of these beverages were eagerly consumed, the best part was making new friends over a warmly proffered drink or three.

Of course, Georgian hospitality has been a longstanding cultural mainstay that goes well beyond a glass of wine or brandy. While I have not yet experienced the Georgian feast known as a "supra," I have enjoyed sumptuous meals around a table that's been covered with plate after plate of traditional Georgian foods. My understanding of a true supra is wave after wave of food accompanied by never ending glasses of home made wines, endless toasts, and lots of music.

The marvelous thing about Georgia, was that every morsel of food, whether it was a casual snack, sit down meal, or specialty of the house prepared at dinner parties, was always something new, intriguing, and worthy of further investigation. Everything was an exotic and flavorful adventure that captivated every one of my senses.

While I reveled in it all, there were a few dishes that stood out. Based on my love of all things dumpling, it should be no surprise that the dish originating in the mountainous regions of Georgia was one of my highlights. Known as khinkali, these are generously sized dumplings filled with either lamb or beef. Of course, there are more contemporary versions filled with either mushrooms, potatoes, or cheese that are equally enticing. Remarkably similar to the Chinese soup-filled dumplings known as xiao long bao, I could eat these all day long.

I also found that Georgia has a remarkable history and talent for cheesemaking. While I have only scratched the surface, slowly discovering new varieties over time, the one that I found most memorable so far is sulgani. At every meal, there is always a plate of this slightly salty and somewhat sour white cheese accompanied by a basket of freshly baked bread. This alone, with a good bottle of wine, would be enough to make a very satisfying meal. Of course, I know of a few cheese shops full of Georgian varieties that could rival any cheese cave in Paris. It goes without saying that a more extensive investigation of Georgian cheeses is on my bucket list.

On every visit, it seemed that the obsession I brought to the table regarding food was a bit unusual. Questions that I'd raise about ingredients, recipes, and methods of preparation were often answered with limited detail or dismissed with an unknowing shrug. Thanks to the internet, and growing interest in Georgian cuisine, I have been able to learn more.

One of the most remarkable dishes I encountered was prasi. A traditional Georgian dish made with leeks, walnuts and garnished with pomegranate arils, prasi was far too intriguing to ignore. With a little bit of investigation, trial, and error at home, I have taught myself how to make something comparable. While a return visit to Georgia to continue my culinary education in the company of local chefs would be preferable, settling for close seconds based on recipes uncovered online will do for now.

The sad truth is that, without meaningful conversations with Georgian chefs, I found it difficult to understand Georgian foodways. Recognizing that there is a growing interest among mainstream media and revealing articles about Georgian cuisine are appearing from time to time, I am slowly gaining an appreciation for the foods I encountered first-hand.

This being said, there was one food rarely sold in stores but regularly displayed by street vendors that had me intrigued. At first glance, I thought these long, somewhat waxy looking things hanging by strings might be hand-crafted candles. I subsequently learned these richly colored tapers were actually a form of confectionery known as churchkhela.

Often referred to as Georgian "Snickers," churchkhela are made by stringing together a dozen or more hazelnuts, then repeatedly dipping the string of nuts into a thick confectionery made from fruit juice and flour. Seeing them prepared at a weekend market, the process is identical to candle making. When enough of a coating has accumulated around the nuts and has fully dried, they are ready to eat. Since the confectionery can be made from any number of juices, churchkhela are available in a variety of flavors and come in an assortment of colors including deep purple, rich mahogany, and dark red. While I enjoyed those bought from various street vendors, the ones that had been machine wrapped and sold in souvenir shops for tourists were nowhere near as good.

I remain hopeful that I'll return to Georgia at least one more time. While I will certainly get my fill of khinkali, khachapuri, cheese and wine, I am ready to investigate further, learn more about the cuisine from local chefs, and get better acquainted with the remarkable variety of foods this country has to offer.

# CHAKHOKHBILI
## (Georgian Chicken & Tomato Stew)
Serves 4

---

*INGREDIENTS*
2 tablespoons olive oil
1 cup onion, diced
6 cloves garlic, finely diced
1 birdseye chili, finely diced
1 lb. chicken, cut into 1/2-inch cubes
1 1/2 cups plum tomatoes, diced
1 teaspoon Khmeli-Suneli*
1 teaspoon sugar
1 teaspoon salt
1/2 teaspoon black pepper
2 tablespoons fresh basil, roughly chopped
2 tablespoons fresh cilantro, roughly chopped

*DIRECTIONS*
Sautee the onion, garlic and red chili pepper until just soft.
Add the chicken and continue cooking for about 5 minutes.

Stir in the tomatoes, followed by the Khmeli-Suneli, sugar,
salt, and black pepper. Reduce heat to a simmer and continue
cooking for 10 minutes.

Add the basil and cilantro and cook for 10 minutes longer.

Adjust seasoning, to taste.

Serve while hot.

*Khmeli-Suneli is a spice blend unique to Georgia. To find, try
ethnic grocery stores or even Georgia restaurants.

# CHICKEN CUTLETS WITH WALNUT SAUCE
## Serves 8

---

*INGREDIENTS*
Walnut Sauce
3 tablespoons sunflower oil
1 cup onion, finely chopped
1 1/2 cups walnut halves
4 cloves garlic, coarsely chopped
1 tablespoon French marigold powder
1 teaspoon blue fenugreek
1 teaspoon ground coriander
1 teaspoon Kosher salt
1 1/2 cups chicken stock

Chicken Cutlets
1 cup flour
1/2 teaspoon salt
1/2 teaspoon pepper
4 chicken breasts chicken, skinless and boneless
1 egg
1/4 cup milk
1 cup breadcrumbs
peanut oil, for frying

For Garnish
1/4 cup chopped walnuts

*DIRECTIONS*
To make the sauce, heat the oil in a small frying pan, add the onions and sauté until soft, about 5 minutes. Using a blender, combine the sautéed onions, walnuts, garlic, French marigold, fenugreek, coriander, and salt. Add the stock, a little at a time,

until everything is well blended. Transfer the sauce to a small pot and keep warm over low heat.

To prepare the chicken, cut each breast in half flat-wise, creating 8 thin cutlets. Pound thinner, as needed, to create uniform thickness across each piece.

Mix the flour, salt and pepper together in one bowl. Beat the egg and milk together in a second bowl. Place the bread-crumbs in a third bowl. Dredge each chicken cutlet first in the flour, then the egg mixture, and lastly in the breadcrumbs. Place the breaded cutlets on a clean plate and set aside.

Pour enough peanut oil into a straight-walled sauté pan to make a 1/4-inch layer. Over medium-high heat, fry each cutlet until they are fully cooked and browned on both sides, then transfer to a paper towel to drain.

To serve, place each cutlet on a plate, then spoon a generous portion of sauce over top. Garnish with chopped walnuts.

# PRASI - GEORGIAN LEEK SALAD
## Serves 8 - 10

*INGREDIENTS*
3 lb. leeks
1 tablespoon salt
6 oz. walnuts
2 tablespoons fresh parsley, finely chopped
2 tablespoons fresh coriander, finely chopped
3 garlic cloves, minced
1/2 teaspoon crushed red pepper
1 teaspoon dry coriander
5 tablespoons white wine vinegar
2 tablespoons olive oil
1 pomegranate - arils for garnish

*DIRECTIONS*
Trim both ends of the leeks, cut in half lengthwise and in half again crosswise. Using a colander, carefully wash the cut leeks, making sure that all of the grit has been removed.

Fill a large pot with water, add the salt and bring to a boil. Add the leeks, reduce to simmer, then cover and cook until tender, about 15 minutes. Drain completely and allow to cool. Squeeze the cooled leeks with your hands to remove as much water as possible, then chop to a coarse texture.

Using a food processor, grind the walnuts into a fine meal, then transfer to a large mixing bowl. Add the parsley, coriander, garlic, pepper, coriander, vinegar and oil and mix thoroughly, followed by the leeks. Add salt to taste, then refrigerate for at least 1 hour.

Garnish with pomegranate arils before serving.

# AFTERWORD
## A few final thoughts.

My work continues to take me to places I would never dream of visiting. Of course, it goes without saying that, on each trip, I always endeavor to learn and enjoy as much as possible about the local cuisine and exotic ingredients.

As I take steps to finish and publish this book, I am unsure whether it will be well received or simply dismissed as an exercise in vanity. For me, it's been a labor of love and one of fond reminiscence - making me realize just how significant the role food has played throughout my life, from those early years in the kitchen with my Mom until, well, right now.

I hope you've found a few of the passages in this book at least a little bit interesting and engaging, or perhaps even slightly entertaining. Perhaps I've provoked your curiosity and you'll visit some of the places I've described on your own, seeking out the foods I found so compelling. Better still, go someplace new and different and share your own stories and recipes with friends and family and write a book of your own.

I also hope that you'll go back through these pages and give some of my recipes a try. I've tested them all, endeavoring to make them easy to understand and simple to prepare.

There are quite a few dishes that are my absolute favorites including Crab Cakes, Biscuits & Gravy, Potato Salad, and Dim Sum (I go for dumplings in any shape or size - just bring 'em on). Of course, let's not forget Macaroni & Cheese, Flourless Chocolate Cake, Fettuccine al Ragu (or Pappardelle) and Welsh Rarebit. Were I a condemned man, a last supper that includes all of these dishes accompanied by a few kilos of steamed lobster and some creamy mashed potatoes would be a delicious way to go.

It would be inappropriate for me to simply eat and run without giving thanks. If you were one of the lucky few who spent time with my Mom and enjoyed one of her fabulous meals, you'll understand why this book would never have happened without her influence, love and support. My Dad too - although I doubt his teaching me how to make a mayonnaise sandwich counts for much (sorry Dad).

It's very important for me to acknowledge all of the people I've worked with in the international development community around the world. Were it not for you, very little in this book would have been possible. To all of you, my heartfelt thanks.

There are also a few cherished friends that I've been cooking, drinking, laughing, and crying with for many years. These are the ones who have endured the ebbs and flows of my culinary career, cooked with me in the kitchen, shared recipes and cooking tips, and spent many a night on the town indulging in every manner of edible or drinkable substances. To all of you, especially Dara B. and Terry R., I say thank you from the bottom of my heart.

# RECUPES